Editorial

ELAINE GRAHAM AND KATE PEARSON

One of the delights of working with women theologians is the sense of community that often comes through conversation. This is due to the intrinsic value that is placed on story and experience in this growing field of research. Every article in this issue of *Crucible*, where we explore lives of women and the changing world of gender and religion, has been birthed from generous conversation. The stories shared are rich and personal and several of our contributors have taken risks in their articles, recognising that by sharing our vulnerabilities and 'daring greatly' (to borrow a phrase from Brené Brown's book of the same name), we can help one another to reflect deeply and discover flourishing for ourselves and society.

Elaine Graham, Grosvenor Research Professor at the University of Chester picks up this theme of storying as she reflects back on a book that changed her. She remembers her first burgeoning bookshelf of theological texts and selects Rosemary Radford Ruether's book, *Sexism and God-Talk* (1983) and its ground-breaking challenge to take the experiences and perspectives of women seriously. Elaine reminds us that those working to bring to voice the experiences of all people who are still marginalised within 'social, gendered and religious hierarchies' are building on the work of many who have gone before. Sara Ahmed speaks of citation as "...feminist memory. It is how we leave a trail of where we have been and who helped us along the way" (Ahmed 2015). So, Elaine helps us to look back and remember; to find our voice that calls to one another for transformation. Ruether's gift to us from nearly forty years ago is a treasure that is still painfully relevant today as it points to environmental crisis, anti-Semitism and racism and challenges us to keep listening to diverse voices for 'theological authenticity'.

Grace Heaton is a DPhil Candidate in the History Faculty at Lincoln College, University Oxford. Grace takes up the quest of

Editorial

'citation as feminist memory' in her exploration of the campaign for women's ordination in the Church of England. Grace brings a fresh voice and perspective to the stories of some of the remarkable women involved in the campaign up to 1994. She explores the language and liturgy of the group Women in Theology, and reminds us of the hard work, resilience and prophetic voices of women who experienced abuse and for whom poetry and inclusive liturgy became 'food for the journey to keep going'. It may feel a lifetime ago, and shocking to recall, that women priests were compared to 'pork pies' but this is still comparatively recent history, and constitutes part of the story of the struggle for women's equality - and recognition in the church. It is a stark reminder of the journey walked so far but also of the path that still rises up ahead for those of us who long for church leadership to reflect the beautiful diversity of humanity.

Dawn Llewellyn, Senior Lecturer in Christian Studies at the University of Chester, continues our theme of storying and citing those who have gone before. She takes us through a deeply personal 'awakening' of herself through the reading of Alice Walker's *The Color Purple* as an undergraduate. Dawn makes herself vulnerable to us, the reader, giving us space to also reflect on the stories and writings of our past that have shaped us and that, whilst we make articulate very differently now, were moments of intense formation that opened a new chapter in our theological journeys.

More courageous vulnerability enables Gill Frigerio to build on the 'moment of awakening' that Dawn describes so eloquently, to bring us right up to date. Gill's article explores the intersectionality of identity and our developing understanding of gender. Gill is an Associate Professor at the University of Warwick, specialising in career development and the working lives of women. In her article she enters into conversation with herself, reflecting on the place of feminism within the church and wider culture today. Gill challenges herself to explore a generous approach to gender, which values the lives and stories of every person. Her self-reflection is remarkably honest; rich and deeply challenging. Gill challenges us to keep looking for the 'transformative nature' of our beliefs and pushes us on to continue to listen for the stories of the other.

Four women and the stories of many before them, invite us in to engage, reflect and prepare for further transformative action that takes seriously the diverse and complex experiences of humankind and dares to hope for more. This is an issue of *Crucible* that focuses on the

Editorial

Elaine Graham and Kate Pearson — 3

Articles

Books That Changed Me: *Sexism and God-Talk* — 6
by Rosemary Radford Ruether
Elaine Graham

'The Male God Blessed the Male Patriarchy': — 14
Language, Ritual and the History of Women's Ordination
Grace Heaton

Books That Changed Me: *The Color Purple* by Alice Walker — 26
Dawn Llewellyn

Talking Gender and Liberation:
Towards a Generous Christian Social Ethic of Gender — 31
Gill Frigerio

Forum

A History of Brexit. Review Essay — 42
Matt Bullimore

Book Reviews

Susannah Cornwall, Karen O'Donnell, Deborah Casewell, — 50
E. S. Kempson, Peter Manley Scott

Crucible is published quarterly by Hymns Ancient & Modern Ltd.
Registered Charity No. 270060

This publication is in collaboration with the Church of England's
Division of Mission and Public Affairs; the William Temple Foundation.

Editorial board
Stephen Platten, Edward Cardale, Kate Pearson, Elaine Graham,
Malcolm Brown, Chris Swift, Carol Wardman,
Matt Bullimore, James Woodward, Peter Scott, Andrew Hayes
(Reviews Editor) and Anna Lawrence (Managing Editor).

Correspondence and articles
Correspondence and articles for submission should be sent to Anna
Lawrence at Hymns Ancient and Modern, anna@hymnsam.co.uk.
Articles should be of about 3,000 words.
Books for review to should be sent to Dr Andrew Hayes,
The Queen's Foundation, Somerset Road, Birmingham, B15 2QH.

Subscriptions
(for four copies): individual rate £22; institutions £30;
international (includes airmail) £40. Single copies cost £7.
All prices included postage and packing. Cheques should
be made payable to Crucible, and sent to: Crucible subscriptions,
Subscription Manager, 13a Hellesdon Park Road, Norwich NR6 5DR.

Tel: 01603 785 910   Fax: 01603 624483.
crucible@hymnsam.co.uk

Direct Debit forms available from the same address

ISSN 0011-2100
ISBN 978-0-334-0596-2

lives of women and the experiences of gender in society but it raises possibilities that reach well beyond. In these narratives and reflections lie the tantalising invitations of liberation and transformation for us all.

Professor Elaine Graham
Grosvenor Research Professor, University of Chester

The Revd Kate Pearson
Anglican Chaplain, University of Warwick

Reference

Ahmed, S. 2015, *Feminist Shelters*, https://feministkilljoys.com/2015/12/30/feminist-shelters/ accessed on 20th February 2020

Books That Changed Me

Sexism and God-Talk by Rosemary Radford Ruether

Elaine Graham

In the early 1980's, I worked for the Student Christian Movement as one of its regional officers. Although I had no formal theological training then, I was passionate about encouraging SCM members and supporters to adopt a thoughtful and intelligent approach to their faith, just as (I hoped) they would do to their studies.

But this meant that I was, essentially, facilitating the theological education of others while undertaking a journey of theological discovery of my own. One of the unexpected privileges of working for SCM (the student body) was to discover its links with SCM Press (the publishing house). SCM Press had originally been founded by its student members, and was by then largely independent but thanks to the benevolence of its Trustees and its Managing Editor, John Bowden, some financial benefits still accrued to the student organisation, including a book discount for its staff. This essentially enabled me to begin to build up a theological library, amongst which were a considerable number of titles in the emerging field of Feminist Theology.

Feminist theology is 'a critical theology of liberation engaged in the reconstruction of theology and religion' (Grey, 1989, 89). As a corrective to male-dominated academic theology, feminist theology excavates new sources and norms according to which 'talk about God' is constituted. Among those early books, *Sexism and God-Talk*, by the American Roman Catholic feminist theologian Rosemary Radford Ruether, still stands as one of the most significant works in the field. *Sexism and God-Talk* was the first systematic exposition of Christian theology from a feminist perspective, dealing with major doctrines of God, Christology, cosmology, theodicy, ecclesiology and eschatology. It still stands the test of time as a foundational text. Ruether's achievement was to expose the partial and ideological nature of theological discourse and then to set out a more inclusive and emancipatory version. She revealed something of the inner workings or historiography of the making of what we call 'tradition' and questioned some of the grounds for what counts as authoritative and authentic within theology.

As a piece of writing, it is both thoroughly scholarly and highly creative and imaginative in style. It draws on an eclectic range of sources: Ancient Near Eastern cosmogonies, Greek myth and philosophy, minority strands of Christianity, Hebrew Bible and New Testament; women's religious writings from antiquity to the present day; contemporary liturgical materials. Ruether insists on the capacity of such sacred texts to admit many forms of exegesis, interpretation, reinterpretation and discursive commentary; a model she draws from the Rabbinic textual traditions of Midrash. So the book begins with a 'Feminist Midrash' – perhaps reflecting Ruether's earlier work on Judaism and the anti-Semitic roots in Christianity – 'The Kenosis of the Father: a feminist *midrash* on the Gospel in three Acts'. It represents an alternative reading of the Christian story, told in part through the witness of Mary Magdalene, as she predicts that the iconoclasm of Jesus of Nazareth will be stifled and institutionalised by his male disciples.

Indeed, part of the critical task of feminist theology is to ask what has happened to what Elizabeth Schüssler Fiorenza termed the 'dangerous memory' of Jesus, as Christian tradition has taken shape over the centuries. Ruether wishes to know whether the Church has remained faithful to that original founding genius of Jesus and his early followers, and how if necessary it can reconnect with that witness. In the process, Ruether undertakes a programme of *critique and reconstruction* of Western Christian theology, asking what counts as relevant and authoritative tradition and challenging the insufficiency of a tradition which has suppressed women's voices and contributions. She then embarks on a reconstructive path, in dialogue with an extended repertoire of sources and voices.

There is an essential hermeneutic guiding and uniting Ruether's twin processes of critique and reconstruction.[1] It rests in the critical principle or criterion of feminist theology as that which promotes the 'full humanity of women': 'whatever diminishes or denies the full humanity of women must be presumed not to reflect the divine or authentic relation to the divine, or to reflect the authentic nature of things, or to be the message or work of an authentic redeemer or a community of redemption.' (Ruether, 1993, 18-19)

The distinctiveness of *feminist* theology, argues Ruether, rests not in its use of experience *per se* but in its attention to the virtually total absence of *women's* experience from the theological canon. This realisation, she argued, 'explodes as a critical force, exposing classical theology, including its codified traditions, as based on *male* experience rather than universal human experience. Feminist theology makes the sociology of theological knowledge visible, no longer hidden behind mystifications of objectified divine and universal authority.'(Ruether, 1993, 13)

Ruether's selection of 'women's experience' as central to feminist theological method is perhaps her best known and most debated. Her argument is that classical theology conceals its origins in what it portrays as a codification of universal human experience; but what passes for objective truth is essentially an ideological reflection of the thought of privileged, first-world men. 'God did not just speak once upon a time to a privileged group of males in one part of the world, making us ever after dependent on the codification of their experience.'(Ruether, 1993, xiv)

Ruether's claim is significant on two counts. First, it draws attention to the rootedness of all theology in experience; and second, it exposes the partial and one-sided nature of what has, up till now, counted as universal experience. Central to this is her view that while the received tradition as constructed and handed down has predominantly reflected male privilege and power, there are compelling alternative strands to what we consider as 'tradition' which proclaim liberation and human dignity for all, represented by the person and work of Jesus Christ. Taking Jesus' self-identification with the prophetic tradition of the Hebrew Bible, his ministry of healing and forgiveness and his flouting of social conventions, including the divisions of gender, religion, ritual purity and economic status, a reading of the Gospels emerges of one who preaches a just and loving God and whose iconoclastic ministry forged a new community in which temporal divisions of status and power were overthrown.

Ruether then turns to what she calls the 'usable tradition' of sources for a renewed and inclusive feminist theology. These comprise authoritative resources or aspects of religious/cultural heritage that might be deployed in augmenting and reforming classical Christianity in order better to realize the values enshrined in her norms. Sources from the usable tradition for her reconstructive task are as follows: first, the prophetic tradition embodied in Scripture, both Hebrew Bible and Christian New Testament, insofar as its canon bears witness to the principles of emancipation outlined above.

The Biblical literature is not adequate on its own, and has to be supplemented by other sources. These include heterodox or 'heretical' strands of Christian tradition such as Gnosticism, Montanism, Quakerism and Shakerism; feminist interpretations of orthodox Christian doctrine; 'pagan' and non-Christian sources such as Goddess, pre-Christian, earth-centred spiritualities; Near Eastern and Greco-Roman religions; and critical post-Christian world-views, such as Marxism, liberalism and feminism. While all these traditions are to some degree compromised by patriarchy, they nevertheless offer what Ruether terms 'intimations of alternatives' by which existing conventions might be critiqued and rejuvenated. In particular, this 'tradition within the tradition' highlights elements such as Jesus' exemplary friendships with, and ministry towards, marginalised persons, especially women; the egalitarian practices of the early Christians (reminiscent of the work of Elizabeth Schüssler Fiorenza in New Testament studies), the radical and counter-cultural visions of prophetic movements throughout the history of Christianity; and post-Christian philosophies such as humanism, romanticism and liberalism.

Ruether thus advances a method for reclaiming lost tradition, countering the terms on which 'orthodoxy' might once have been drawn up, in the name of restoring the silenced and marginalized theological voices of women and others. Crucially, however, she would insist that this is simply a matter of clarifying the essential message of the Gospel – which runs like a 'golden thread' throughout Christian history – of liberative, egalitarian and prophetic teaching.

Running throughout Ruether's work is a deep concern to end injustice in religious and social institutions, practices and structures. Her critical analysis is directed at a dualistic and distorted cultural imagination premised on difference and hierarchy rather than mutual relationality. The root of this is the characterisation of women as *Other*, the one who deviates from the masculine norm and is therefore secondary or inferior. This is systemic and tied into other binary and hierarchical ways of ordering the world.

In contrast to this deep cultural dualism in which male and female appear virtually as separate species, rests a parallel, contradictory anthropology which conceives of 'the equivalence of maleness and femaleness in the image of God' (Ruether, 1993, 93). Yet this has been suppressed in favour of a patriarchal model of humanity which regards women as inferior, misbegotten and subordinate. If women have laboured under the stigma of being the 'Other' to androcentric projections of reality, then feminist theory and theology has had to work out how to speak about women's lived experiences in ways that disclose their epistemological and phenomenological complexity without losing political and analytical coherence.

What does the achievement of 'full humanity' really look like? Critics have often argued that to root her theological method in a hermeneutics of experience reduces it simply to a form of humanistic sociology of knowledge. Not so. Together with other feminist theologians of her generation, including Mary Daly and Judith Plaskow, Ruether insists, in the worlds of Plaskow, that 'the right question is theological' (Plaskow, 1983, 226). In other words, the vision of a fuller humanity requires the renewal and reorientation of our images of divinity, free from patriarchy and dualism. Ruether coins the use of the term God/ess to express this synthesis of both male and female forms of the divine.

The category of 'women's experience' has been of revolutionary and untold value for feminist theory and politics. Yet it almost goes without saying that at the instant of its assertion and declamation comes an apprehension of its limitations: which women? Under what circumstances? How is it expressed? What are the origins of such differential experience? The danger is, as Kwok Pui-lan argues, that it reproduces the patterns of colonialism:

> The appeal to universal human experience and the inability to respect diverse cultures are expressions of a colonizing motive: the incorporation of the Other into one's own culture or perspective. (Pui-lan, 2005, 56)

As feminist theory has grown in significance and became more diverse, so too it has been recognised that whatever its strategic significance, the currency of such an appeal to a trans-cultural, generic concept has been undermined by the risk of its perpetuation of the 'original sin' of universalising diverse and pluralistic lives. The matrices of race, class, dis/ability, education, religion and sexual orientation have been vital tools in understanding the complex dynamics of global and cross-cultural patterns of power and difference. While Ruether's work has come in for criticism for its implicit failure to accommodate the diversity of feminist theological discourse, therefore, she would be the first to acknowledge that she is but one voice among many and that however partial her own stand-point as a white, Roman Catholic, married, North American academic, any attempt to speak from a universal or neutral stand-point would simply reinforce the ideological patterns of patriarchal knowledge. For Ruether, one can only write from experience, wise to the implications of the sociology of knowledge in locating and limiting one's epistemology, but nevertheless striving for 'the acknowledgement of cultural particularity in solidarity with others in their distinctiveness.' (Ruether, 1993, xvi)

Part of Ruether's intellectual exercise as an historian has been to identify the pervasive extent of binary systems of thinking: not only gender, but race, class and, critically, human attitudes to non-human nature. She was one of the first feminist theologians to recognise how the invidious adoption of binary dualisms extends to relations between humanity and non-human nature. While this strand of her thinking is more fully developed elsewhere, in works such as *New Woman, New Earth* (1975) and *Gaia and God* (1992), the analysis in *Sexism and God-Talk* of the prevalence of social, gendered and religious hierarchies also gestures towards this ultimate system of dominance, that of humanity over nature. The feminisation of nature and 'naturalisation' of women are presented as part of an integrated pattern of social domination. Similarly, as well as pointing to the connection between 'the mistreatment of women and the mistreatment of nature', Ruether's entire intellectual endeavour reveals a connection between patterns of thought (or ideology) and material relations in society. She engages in holistic and anti-dualistic thinking that connects sexism, environmental crisis, racism, anti-Semitism and other hierarchies as part of an interlocking cultural imaginary. How we conceive of the world – even and especially down to what we elevate as our G/gods – will have a bearing on how social groups are privileged, subjugated, enriched or impoverished.

To summarise, Ruether's work is advanced within a strong ethical and political framework, in which theological discourse serves a purpose, which is not to enshrine the insights of the past or support beliefs and practices that reinforce human inequality and domination, but to testify to the spirit of God in Jesus who preached a message of liberation. We might also note her constant reference to the 'prophetic' traditions enshrined in Hebrew Bible, in the person and work of Jesus and counter-cultural social movements. For Ruether, this is a bed-rock, and represents a call to radical repentance which is both a change of heart and blueprint for transformed practice. Such a transformation does not simply aim at an inversion of sexism or discrimination, but is an attempt to realise 'a continually expanding definition of inclusive humanity – inclusive of both genders, inclusive of all social groups and races.'(Ruether, 1993, 20).

This vision of liberation comprises God's preferential option for the poor, a critique of ideological religion that sanctifies particular versions of human experience in order to justify discrimination, and a dismantling of dualistic and hierarchical models of power. It embodies a vision of a new age to come, prefigured in the practices of those who identify with the prophetic imagination of Hebrew Bible, early Christianity and even many 'secular' progressive social movements.

The significance of this book has been to alert churches and theology to the historical exclusion of women from the tradition, but also to the centrality of gender to the activities of ministry, the language of religious experience and theological discourse, and the importance of religious symbolism in shaping predominant representations of gender in Western culture (Ruether, 2010). Ruether does not attempt to claim that feminist theology is simply a specialist or partisan branch of 'real' theology. Rather, her book taught me that a feminist framework of critique and reconstruction should reveal what all theology, and all good theology should do, which was to acknowledge and address the particularity of its context, exercise transparency and rigour towards its core sources and articulate the relevance of 'God-talk' for the life of the Church and the world. We shouldn't miss, either, the claim that all theology is essentially culturally-specific. Ruether reminds us that it is codified human knowledge, only a series of culturally-bound, linguistically- and symbolically-mediated representations of the divine. This signals the significance of contextual knowledge for theological understanding and reminds theologians that no talk about God can ever be final or absolute.

Eventually, my original copy of *Sexism and God-Talk* fell apart due to constant use. I still use it in teaching and research to this day, because it continues to serve both as an historical record of the early stages of feminist theology and as a manifesto for its continuing work and significance. At the heart of its enduring value is the claim that by listening to the distinctive voices and spiritual journeys of women, feminist theology can expose and resist the sexism embedded in theological language, ecclesiastical authority, liturgical and pastoral practice. If theological authenticity resides in that which promotes the full humanity of all people and affords their experiences of the divine some visibility within received tradition and agency, then we can see how feminist theology is necessary for the renewal of the life of the Church and Christian practice.

Elaine Graham is Grosvenor Research Professor at the University of Chester

Note

1. Throughout Ruether's work, we can see this same commitment to dialectical thinking, as in the titles of so many of her books which juxtapose the oppressive and the liberative, informed by that same framework of critique and reconstruction: *Faith and Fratricide* (1972), *Sexism and God-Talk* (1983), *New Woman, New Earth* (1975), *Gaia and God* (1992), *America, Amerikkka* (2014).

References

Grey, Mary C., 1989, *Redeeming the dream: feminism, redemption and Christian tradition.* London: SPCK.

Plaskow, Judith, 1983, "The right question is theological." In S. Heschel, ed. *On being a Jewish feminist*, New York: Schocken Books, pp. 224-227.

Pui-lan, Kwok, 2005, *Postcolonial Imagination and Feminist Theology.* London: SCM.

Ruether, Rosemary Radford, 1993, *Sexism and God-Talk: Toward a Feminist Theology* (2nd edn., first published 1983), Boston: Beacon Press.

Ruether, R. R., 2010, 'Feminist Theology: where is it going?' *International Journal of Public Theology* 4.1, pp. 5-20.

'The Male God Blessed the Male Patriarchy'

Language, Ritual and the History of Women's Ordination

GRACE HEATON

'That night we gathered for the birth, as women
have always done - as women
have never done till now;
and in an ordinary room,
warm, exposed, and intimate as childbed,
we spoke about our bodies and our blood,
waiting for God's delivery:
silence, gesture, and speech
announcing, with a strange appropriate blend
of mystery and bluntness
the celebration of the word made flesh
midwived wholly by women.'

'That night we gathered'
Janet Morley, *All Desires Known*, 1988. p.108.

On Christmas Eve 1986 members of Women in Theology (WIT) gathered in the lounge of Holy Trinity House, an Anglican Franciscan house in Paddington, London, to celebrate the Eucharist. Together the group reflected upon the birth of Christ. They recalled the blood of Mary's womb which nourished the unborn child and the milk that later fed Him at her breast. The rituals of motherhood led Mary to perform the ultimate Eucharistic act of feeding and nourishing Christ with her body and her blood, which in turn became Christ's redemptive blood. Generations of mothers, like Mary, baked bread to nourish the bodies and souls of those closest to them. Yet, these same women were denied the opportunity to break the Eucharistic bread (Slee, 78).

This article explores both the power of words and the entwined nature of language and liberation. For those campaigning for women's ordination in the Church of England, changing attitudes towards women, and their roles and status within church life, was as imperative as changing laws and legislation. This article examines the complexities associated with challenging the traditionally masculine language used to describe God, and situates those individuals experimenting with inclusive language and creative liturgies within the wider campaigns for women's ordination. It draws upon my doctoral research, which involves conducting oral history interviews with individuals, both male and female, lay and clerical, involved in the campaign for women's ordination between 1968-1994. Interviewees frequently emphasis the importance of finding communities, like WIT, which affirmed women's lived experiences as holy and sacred. These communities sought to conceive of new, more inclusive ways of worshipping. Books like *All Desires Known*, an influential book of prayers, collects and psalms, were born out of a longing felt by many women for a language of worship that was inclusive of women's experiences whilst simultaneously being rooted in the words, stories and images of Scripture.

Inspiration was drawn from psalms such as psalm 22: 9–10 in which God is envisaged as a caring midwife,

> Yet you drew me out of the womb,
> you entrusted me to my mother's breasts;
> placed on your lap from my birth,
> from my mother's womb you have been my God.[1]

The space in which women give birth has traditionally been a female domain, and in casting God as an active and present figure within the birthing chamber, this psalm demonstrates that God is concerned with both the physical and spiritual dynamics of birth. Images like this were built upon by activists, such as theologian Nicola Slee, who sought to 'reclaim women's bodies and blood as holy and capable of expressing the life of God' therefore challenging 'the idea that the

Language, Ritual and the History of Women's Ordination

body and blood of Jesus is holy and sacred but the bodies and blood of women are not'.[2] For those raised in communities in which God was spoken about in exclusively male terms, as 'Father', 'Lord' and 'Master', inclusive language could be a revelation. Janet Morley, one of the key architects of inclusive language, explained,

> I had been brought up on the patriarchal stories from the Bible, the patriarchal language of the Church, the male priesthood, the authority of my father within the family, the authority of males within University and workplace and so on. It was all coherent and everything fitted. The sort of male God sort of blessed the male patriarchy and actually when you started to ask questions about that, things didn't fit in the same way, they were disrupted and that was both very exciting and quite uncomfortable.[3]

The sense of discomfort articulated by Janet Morley was echoed by other women who described the unease they felt when speaking about God in the feminine. Altering words can profoundly change the meaning of what is said, and for many changing 'He' to 'She' meant deconstructing previously unchallenged and often unexplored ideas about God. Whilst certain alteration to religious language were easily implemented, such as swapping 'mankind' to 'humankind', changing the language used to speak about God was a complicated task. Groups like WIT encouraged individuals to stay with their sense of discomfort, to explore what could be learnt about both themselves and God within that uneasiness.

Using feminine language for God, with all its difficulties and complexities, demonstrated that all language for God is inadequate and can only hope to point to what is ineffable. Traditionally unchallenged masculine language for God merely presented an illusion of adequacy. Yet, for many women disrupting entrenched ideas surrounding the maleness of God proved to be exceedingly difficult. Rachel Carr explained 'using female language as a metaphor for God didn't mean I had ceased to imagine God in my head as a man with a white beard' (The St Hilda Community, 20). Many advocates of inclusive language also spoke honestly about the inelegance and awkwardness that resulted in attempting to remove gender from religious language. In 1991 Monica Furlong, a religious affairs correspondent and a radical advocate for women's ordination, commented, 'I should hate to see "God rest ye merry, gentlemen" modernised to some ideologically sound equivalent' (Furlong, 84).

Media discussions about inclusive language seemed to paradoxically insist that the issue was too trivial to be disused and, on the other hand, that to raise it was positively satanic (Morley, 60). Within the 'Letters Page' of the *Church Times* the campaign for female ordination was described as 'the work of the Devil', and the motivation for inclusive language condemned as a 'rebellion against God'. Women who experimented with creative liturgy and inclusive language in the 1970s and 1980s frequently described their endeavours as feeling 'transgressive' and 'subversive'.[4] Despite the radicalism and controversy associated with this reclamation of religious language, women since the Medieval era have used feminine images and metaphors to describe God. One such woman was the mystic Julian of Norwich, who wrote *Revelations of Divine Love* the first work in English to be authored by a woman. In it, she recalled sixteen visions that took place in May 1373, whilst she was gravely ill. She wrote,

> The human mother will suckle her child with her own milk, but our beloved Mother Jesus, feeds us with himself, and, with the most tender courtesy, does it by means of the blessed Sacrament. (Walters, chapter 60).

This image, which combines both the femininity of God with the ritual of breastfeeding has been a source of inspiration for women who have longed for language which reflects both their God, and their lived experience. Booklets of worship material such as *Celebrating Women*, published in 1986, highlighted the 'continuous act of translation' undertaken by women in order to find themselves 'in a male-orientated discourse' (Ward; Wild; Morley, 6). *Celebrating Women* described this act of translation as an 'irritation and a distraction from worship' and explained that for a number of women 'to be surrounded by exclusive language is a repeated encounter with rejection, precisely in the place where we seek acceptance at the deepest level of our being' (Ward; Wild; Morley, 6).

Celebrating Women emphasised the importance of including silence in worship which used inclusive language. Hearing God referred to as 'Mother', 'Sister' or 'Lover' for the first time could be a very powerful experience and time and space was often needed to digest what was heard. Whilst those campaigning for women's ordination emphasised the importance of inclusive language, they also acknowledged that there are other ways of communicating with one another during worship which transcend the verbal. Silence and symbolism were as important as language and liturgy. Moreover, emotions and meaning were frequently conveyed not through words, but through tone, intonation and body language.

For Janet Morley the Christmas Eve Eucharist, which inspired the poem 'That night we gathered', was particularly meaningful as it was her first experience of a Eucharist presided over by a woman; the Reverend Suzanne Fageol, ordained in 1978 by the Episcopal Church of America. Fageol regularly celebrated the Eucharist in England for women who craved female ministerial leadership. Earlier in the year General Synod voted against the 'Women Lawfully Ordained Abroad' Measure which would have allowed women from other Anglican churches to celebrate the Eucharist in England and Wales. As such, Eucharists like this Christmas Eve celebration were dubbed 'illegal' and those opposed to women's ordination often argued that these celebrations were politically motivated.

However, for many women these private house Eucharists were less statements of affirmation for women's ministry and were instead, what the Reverend Judith Maltby, chaplain at Corpus Christi College, Oxford, has described as, 'our food for the journey, to keep going'.[5] These intimate celebrations gave activists the strength to continue campaigning for women's ordination and enabled many women to continue attending their regular Anglican churches.

The activism surrounding women's ordination reached its zenith in the late 1980s and early 1990s, culminating on 11 November 1992 when the motion to ordain women to the priesthood received the necessary two-thirds majority in the Houses of Bishops, Clergy and Laity. Whilst the first 32 women were ordained as priests at Bristol Cathedral on 12 March 1994 by Bishop Barry Rogerson, the origins of the campaign can be traced back to the nineteenth-century revival in women's ministry. The Church Missionary Society sent their first female missionary abroad in 1820, in 1845 Dr Edward Pusey founded a sisterhood to work in Park Village, London, and in 1862 Elizabeth Ferard became the Church of England's first deaconess of modern times.[6] In 1909 the first Anglican organisation in favour of female ordination was founded, the Church League for Women's Suffrage (CLWS), which was committed to campaigning for women's representation in Parliament and in the councils of the Church.

In his recent article on the 'Religious Routes to Women's Suffrage'

Robert Saunders demonstrated that activists regarded religion as a catalyst for women's emancipation. Saunders suggested that for 'militant' suffragists the struggle for women's political emancipation often acquired a sacramental character. Imprisonment was conceived as a 'baptism' and force-feeding as a 'crucifixion' (Saunders, 2). Moreover, for militant suffragette Annie Kenny the Edwardian suffrage campaign was 'more like a religious revival than a political movement' (Kenny, 298). Christianity thus informed suffrage discourses and practices, whilst campaigns surrounding the advancement of women in public life shaped the ways in which the movement for women's ordination was understood within wider British culture.

By 1918 the *Representation of the People Act*, which gave men aged over 21 and some women aged over 30 the right to vote, had passed through Parliament and the partial aims of the CLWS were achieved. The movement reorganised itself as the League of the Church Militant (LCM) and presented a petition in favour of women's ordination to the 1920 Lambeth Conference. The petition was greeted with incomprehension and the Bishop of Ely described the petition as 'a shock revolution so complete and so perilous' that it had no place in the Conference's remotest vision (Jones, 643). However, the Conference did include 'The Ministrations of Women' on its agenda and women's ministry was discussed at both the 1920 and 1930 Lambeth Conferences.

Two new organisations emerged in the late 1920s; the Anglican Group for the Ordination of Women to the Historic Ministry of the Church (AGOW) formed in 1929, and the Society for the Equal Ministries of Men and Women (SEMW) founded in 1930. As women priests appeared to be a distant dream, AGOW instead focused its attention on the status of deaconesses and the issue of equal lay ministry in the Church.[7] It deliberately refrained from actively campaigning for female priests so as not to alienate their more modest campaign objectives, and to maintain the support of those who were against female ordination but advocated equal lay participation in Church life (Jones, 105).

Whilst the campaigns had somewhat stalled in the Church of England, on 25th January 1944 Florence Li Tim-Oi became the first women to be ordained within the Anglican Communion. During the Japanese occupation of Hong Kong, Florence Li Tim-Oi had been in charge of an Anglican parish in the Portuguese island colony, Macao. When priests were eventually refused their monthly permit to travel

Language, Ritual and the History of Women's Ordination

from Japanese occupied territory to Macao in order to celebrate the Eucharist, the Bishop of Hong Kong, Ronald O. Hall, made the decision to ordain Florence Li Tim-Oi 'as a priest in the Church of God'. He believed that the pastoral needs of the Macanese community were more important than the gender of the priest.[8]

The pair agreed to meet on St Paul's day in the Free China village of Shui Hing, a two or three day journey from Macao and a five day journey for the Bishop on foot and by boat. Remarkably, despite the distances travelled they arrived within twenty minutes of one another. Bishop Hall knew that the ordination of Li Tim-Oi was a momentous step and compared his actions to those of the Apostle Peter when he baptised the Gentile Cornelius. St Peter recognised that God had already given Cornelius the Baptismal gift of the Spirit, and likewise Bishop Hall believed he was merely confirming that God had already given Li Tim-Oi the gift of priestly ministry.[9] Six months later the *Church Times* published the news of Li Tim-Oi's ordination under the headline, 'Bishop in Insurrection'. The article strongly denounced Bishop Hall's actions and urged the Chinese Church to issue a formal and categorical condemnation. In 1946, to defuse the controversy, Li Tim-Oi surrendered her priestly licence, but not her Holy Orders.

Throughout the twentieth century Li Tim-Oi's ordination provided hope to many. Maude Royden, a suffrage feminist and campaigner for women's ordination, wrote to Li Tim-Oi in 1946 and explained, 'I have myself felt the call...to the priesthood and...been refused. When I heard of your ordination...my heart leapt with joy' (Fletcher, 281). But a further 25 years passed before the Anglican Consultative Council, chaired by Archbishop Michael Ramsey, passed Resolution 28 which advised Bishops that, 'with the approval of their province, they might ordain women to the priesthood' (Chan-Yeung, 76). Upon receiving Resolution 28, Bishop Gilbert Baker, Ronald O. Hall's successor, immediately ordained two women, Jane Huang and Joyce Bennett, and reinstated Li Tim-Oi's licence.

By 1974 the Episcopal Church of America had begun ordaining women. Initially, an 'illegal ordination' of eleven women, the 'Philadelphia Eleven', took place on July 1974 before a congregation of over two thousand, and during the following winter a further three women were ordained in Washington. By 1976 the General Convention of the Episcopal Church had voted both to ordain women and to accept the ministry of those women illegally ordained. Canada and New Zealand were quick to follow suit and started ordaining women priests in 1975 and 1976 respectively.

In England by 1978, Una Kroll, a doctor and one of the founders of Christian Parity Group, was hopeful that legislation to allow women to enter the priesthood would be passed by General Synod at their November meeting. Kroll was part of a group that kept an all-night prayer vigil outside Church House where the meeting was to be held. In the morning, Kroll climbed the stairs to the public gallery to watch the debate. As the hostility in the gallery and legislative chamber intensified, Kroll developed an overwhelming sense that the vote was going to fail. Kroll recalled that 'some words came into my mind unbidden and would not leave', and when it was announced that motion had been defeated in the House of Clergy, she stood up with another supporter, Susan Dowell, and shouted 'We asked you for bread and you gave us a stone' (Kroll, 1009).

Opposition to women's ordination was strong and enduring, frequently dehumanising women and their experiences. In the introduction of her edited collection *Voices of This Calling*, Christina Rees, CBE and one-time Chair of WATCH, explained that a minor council met in the fourth century to debate, amongst other things, the question 'are women human?'. Entering into the frenzied debate, Augustine of Hippo concluded that women could be human, but only in their minds and spirits, not their bodies. Similarly, Aristotle in *Generation of Animals* declared 'we should look upon the female state as being as it were a deformity' and in *Summa Theologica* St Thomas Aquinas described woman as defective and misbegotten men (Rees, 20). In 1558 leading Protestant reformer, John Knox, wrote a pamphlet, entitled *The First Blast of the Trumpet against the Monstrous Regiment of Women*, within which he attacked female monarchs arguing that rule by females was contrary to the Bible.

Rees argued that whilst one would hope that these views towards women would have vanished by the late twentieth century, comments made during the debates surrounding women's ordination demonstrated that 'a debased view of women and their bodies still persists at the beginning of the third millennium' (Rees, 20). In a General Synod debate in the late 1980s Graham Leonard, the Bishop of London, described women priests as 'a virus in the bloodstream which could never be got out (Furlong, 119). Likewise, in 1995 a male Anglican priest who decided to become a Roman Catholic said to a Catholic nun, 'I'd rather ordain a cat than a woman' and another Anglican priest stated 'You can no more ordain a woman than you can ordain a pork pie' (Rees, 20).

With every slander and slur, the opposition to women's ordination dehumanised and debased the personhood and contributions of women. Part of the dehumanisation of women in religion, and particularly women involved in the campaigns for women's ordination, was a denial of their emotions and the silencing of their pain. Una Kroll's cry proved to be the last public words she would utter for over seven years. Fighting for women's ordination meant that Una was 'subjected to relentless ridicule from the press and derision and anger from the clergy' (Dowell & Williams 47). She recognised her actions had caused harm to the cause she supported and decided to step away from public life.

Reflecting on the events leading up to 1979 Kroll wrote,

> The reason behind my 'leaving' visible leadership for total commitment to prayer, beginning in 1979, when I left London, [was] that I do not believe in one woman leading and knew that unless many women led and led differently (as they have done) we would never get anywhere.
> (Dowell & Williams 48).

The wider and more collective leadership Kroll envisaged was established on 21st November 1978, mere weeks after the General Synod ruling. A meeting chaired by Dame Betty Ridley, Third Church Estates Commissioner and a distinguished church administrator, embarked upon the process of setting up a national movement to campaign for the ordination of women. The Movement for the Ordination of Women (MOW) was born.

MOW campaigned tirelessly to bring about legislative change to allow women to test their vocations as priests. MOW organised conferences, held prayerful vigils, and arranged celebratory services for important occasions like the 40th anniversary of Florence Li Tim-Oi's ordination, held at Westminster Abbey in 1984. Throughout their campaigning years MOW published prolifically, from books and booklets, to pamphlets and newsletters, seeking to both publicise their cause and educate their readership. MOW was committed to the idea that to bring about real change, attitudes in the Church, as well as its laws, needed to be changed.

Words link us to our ancestry, but those individuals experimenting with inclusive language understood that this could be at the expense of isolating individuals in the present. Whilst religious language is imbued with the beauty and traditions of the past, like all forms of language, it constantly evolves. The tradition of using inclusive language formed the basis for feminist theologians, poets, and writers of today, to reclaim and revisit the lives of women in the Bible with greater vivacity than ever before. From Nicola Slee's anthology of poetry which writes the humanity back into Mary, to Paula Gooder's imaginative retelling of the life of Phoebe, to the Bible Society's podcast *#SheToo* which re-examines the 'texts of terror' in order to give voices to women violated within these passages.

Whilst inclusive language has been a revelation for many women, the feelings of joy and liberation at finding ways to speak about the femininity of God were often sharply contrasted with the pain of feeling unwelcome and under-valued within conventional Anglican Churches. The pain of ostracisation is especially magnified, and experienced all the more acutely by women and non-binary people who are part of the LGBTQIA+ community, a group who continue to suffer through a lack of inclusive language through which a God of unconditional love can be visible and tangible.

Equally urgent and prophetic voices are needed to counter and contend with long-held traditional language that unwittingly permits racism and ableism to persist in communities. Inclusive language, whilst not a cure-all solution, is an important step in encouraging individuals to question their reliance on traditional forms and titles used in prayer and worship. It forces individuals to confront worship in new ways, and seeks to welcome a diverse spectrum of lived experiences.

Grace Heaton is a DPhil Candidate in the History Faculty at Lincoln College, University Oxford. If you were involved in the campaigns for women's ordination and would be happy to be interviewed please do contact grace.heaton@lincoln.ox.ac.uk.

Language, Ritual and the History of Women's Ordination

Notes

1. The Jerusalem Bible.
2. Oral history interview conducted by Grace Heaton with Nicola Slee, 2019.
3. Oral History interview conducted by Grace Heaton with Janet Morley, 2019.
4. Oral History interviews conducted by Grace Heaton with Judith Maltby, 2019.
5. Oral History interview conducted by Grace Heaton with Judith Maltby, 2019.
6. 'The Movement for the Ordination of Women, 1989, Fact Pack May', (6MOW, The Women's Library, LSE).
7. 'Women's Ministry', (The Women's Library, LSE).
8. Oral History interview conducted by Grace Heaton.
9. http://www.ittakesonewoman.org/public/litimoi_story.php

Questions for discussion

1. What images of God do you hold?

2. What are the dangers of universalising women's experience?

3. Can the male imagery of traditional Christology be changed without doing violence to the historical particularity of Christ as a first-century Jew?

References

Chan-Yeung, M., 2015, *The Practical Prophet: Bishop Ronald O. Hall and His Legacies*, Hong Kong: Hong Kong University Press.

Dowell, S. and Williams, J., 1994, *Bread, Wine and Women: The Ordination Debate in the Church of England*, London: Virago Press.

Fletcher, S., 1989, *Maude Royden: A Life*, Oxford: Basil Blackwell.

Furlong, M., 1991, *A Dangerous Delight: Women and Power in the Church*, London, SPCK.

Heeney, B., 1988, *The Women's Movement in the Church of England*, Oxford: Oxford University Press.

Jones, T.W., 2012, '"Unduly Conscious of Her Sex": priesthood, female bodies, and sacred space in the Church of England', *Women's*

Historical Review 21, pp.639-655.
Jones, T. W., 2013, *Sexual Politics in the Church of England, 1857-1957*, Oxford: Oxford University Press
Kenney, A., 1924, *Memories of a Militant*, London. Quoted in, Saunders, R., 2019, ' *"A Great and Holy War": Religious Routes to Women's Suffrage, 1909-1914'*, Oxford: Oxford University Press, pp.1-32.
Mann, R., 2012, *Dazzling Darkness: Gender, Sexuality, Illness and God*, Glasgow: Wild Goose Publications.
Morley, J., 2005, *All Desires Known*, 3rd edn, London: SPCK.
Morley, J. 1984, 'The Faltering Words of Men', in Furlong, M. (ed.) *Feminine in the Church*, London: SPCK.
Rees, C. (ed.), 2002, *Voices of This Calling*, Norwich: Canterbury Press Norwich.
Saunders, R., 2019, *"A Great and Holy War": Religious Routes to Women's Suffrage, 1909-1914*, Oxford: Oxford University Press, pp.1-32.
Slee, N., 2003, *Faith and Feminism: An introduction to Christian Feminist Theology*, London: Darton, Longman and Todd Ltd.
Slee, N., 2007, *The Book of Mary*, London: SPCK.
'The Movement for the Ordination of Women, 1989, Fact Pack May', (6MOW, The Women's Library, LSE).
The St. Hilda Community., 1996, *The New Women Included: A Book of Services and Prayers*, 2nd edn, London: SPCK.
Women's Ministry', (5AGO, The Women's Library, LSE).
Walters, C. (trans.), 1966, *Julian of Norwich, Revelations of Divine Love*, London: Penguin.
Ward, H., Wild, J. and Morley, J. (eds.), 1995, *Celebrating Women*, London: SPCK.

Books That Changed Me

The Color Purple by Alice Walker

Dawn Llewellyn

As any academic researcher and reader will tell you, too many books have inspired my thinking. There are the authors that voice the illusive thread I've been searching for, like when trying to understand the relationship between feminist theology and literature at the start of my PhD, I came across Heather Walton's work, or how Lynne Pearce and Janice Radway helped me develop a feminist approach to religious reading practices. There are authors I'm fortunate to have as friends and colleagues, who weave theory with lived experiences, and I'm grateful for the way scholars like Nicola Slee, Anna Strhan, Anna Fisk, Sonya Sharma, and Marta Trzebiatowska tell stories that bring religious worlds to life. Then there are the authors that have left me slightly disjointed and set me apart from the things I thought I knew and understood. The books where my notes, scribbles, underlining and highlighting record my responses, confusions, and questions (in some, you can barely make out the original text because my annotations and scrawls scratch over the print). The books that felt risky to read because I wasn't quite the same as I was before I had opened up the pages.

My third year of my undergraduate degree is peppered with such reading experiences that at times seemed profound and visceral. I had left the University of Edinburgh for a year, where I was studying Philosophy and Systematic Theology, and travelled to Queen's University in Ontario as an exchange student. Perhaps it was the adventure and novelty of being part of an international programme, in a new country with new courses, lecturers, learning approaches, and classmates but I can still remember how certain key texts made me feel. Reading is, after all, an emotional, implicated relationship between reader, author, text and context that is an interpretive and an embodied, responsive activity (Llewellyn). For example, my copy of Peter Berger's *The Sacred Canopy* is full of my exclamation marks as I started to unravel what it means to say that religion was constructed; Edward Said's *Orientalism* challenged all of my assumptions about colonialism; and Elizabeth Schüssler Fiorenza's *Bread Not Stone* revealed the androcentric and patriarchal production and interpretation of Christianity's sacred texts. However, it was reading Alice Walker's *The Color Purple* in my first feminist theology seminar, in the first week of the school year, which tripped me up.

We had done the usual first class introductions, gone through the course outline, and I was still a bit confused as to what a module in 'Feminist Theology' would cover. Up to this point, (it was the late 1990) I had only been taught by male lecturers and course reading lists didn't feature women philosophers or theologians; to say I had had limited academic exposure to feminism was an understatement. I had taken the course out of curiosity, because it fitted in with my timetable, and I had heard that the course instructor – Professor Pamela Dickey-Young was 'sort of famous'. It was the first time I had been taught by a woman at university.

In that initial class, Prof Young presented us with an extract from *The Color Purple* to discuss. This epistolary novel by the womanist thinker, activist, essayist and novelist Alice Walker features Celie, a 14 year old black girl living in the American south. Celie writes letters to God and to her sister, Nettie, about her life, her unhappy relationship with Alfonso, the man she lives with, who mistreats her, and she believes to be her father. The novel addresses racialized, sexual, and economic violence against Celie and the other women in her community. It also features repeatedly in feminist theology. Carol Christ and Judith Plaskow suggest it is one of the most cited feminist theological texts; Heather Walton discusses its place in the development of feminist theology; Daphne Hampson refers to it as signalling an image of the divine that troubles male images of God; Margaret Kamitsuka notes the importance of the lesbian relationship between Celie and Shug (Celie's friend, confidant, and lover); and Susan Thistlethwaite has dryly noted the frequency with which feminist theologians refer to it. We were reading the oft-cited part of the novel where Shug and Celie discuss their understanding of God, and Shug asks Celie, 'Tell me what your God look like':

> He big and old and tall and graybeareded and white...
> Then she tell me this old white man is the same God she used to see when she prayed. If you want to find God in Church, Celie, she say, that's who is bound to show up, cause that where he live. [...]
> Cause that's the one that's in the white folks' white bible.
> (Walker, 165)

I had read the novel and seen the film adaptation – and loved them – but I was unaware of its popularity in feminist theological thinking. In addition, I had not seen the challenge that the novel posed to this constructed image of God that I had inherited from my Roman Catholic upbringing at Church, school and University. I had only considered God as white, male, and patriarchal, without question. When the class ended, I was confused. My classmates and I left a little dazed following our excited and lively exchanges prompted by the session, and we were wrestling with how to handle the implications this reading experience had for the Christian tradition. I was disorientated and felt a degree of unease. I knew that my political, theological and personal horizon was shifting but I wasn't quite sure how to work through how I had been confronted by my white privilege. In my learning journal – a coursework requirement – I describe my response:

> It is about the experience of women, their everyday living and how this interacts with their spirituality ... [which] has been smothered by male images of a God that does not connect to their life experience...I find that quite disturbing that I had not really thought about this before.

Of course, I now squirm with embarrassment when I read this and think of my 20-year-old self, writing the journal. Although, as Heather Walton points out, the novel is used to illustrate how black women's spiritual heritage is excluded by white feminist theology's cultural and racial essentialism, I am deeply uncomfortable that I was unreflexively at ease with my appropriation of this example of black women naming, critiquing, and theologising their experiences of God. It was, however, as they say, the 'click': a moment of 'awakening' to the ways private and public life are inflected with inequalities relating to gender, race, class, and sexuality. I was angry I had not questioned this before. This encounter introduced me to feminism, feminist theology, the intersections of gender, race, and class, and the power of literature to carve out spaces where the sacred, gendered world can be probed and reimagined. And it also revealed how the experience of reading can cause aftershocks that continue to shape one's academic and spiritual story.

Dawn Llewellyn is Senior Lecturer in Christian Studies at the University of Chester

References

Berger, P. L., 1967, *The Sacred Canopy Elements of a Sociological Theory of Religion*, New York: Anchor Books.

Christ, C., and Plaskow, J., (eds), 1992 [1975], *Womanspirit A Feminist Reader in Religion*, San Francisco: Harper San Francisco.

Fisk. A., 2014, *Sex, Sin and Our Selves: Encounters in Feminist Theology and Contemporary Women's Literature*, Eugene: Wipf and Stock.

Hampson, D., 1990, *Theology and Feminism*. Oxford: Blackwell.

Kamitsuka, M., D., 2007, *Feminist Theology and the Challenge of Difference*. Oxford: Oxford University Press.

Llewellyn, D., 2015, *Reading, Feminism, and Spirituality: Breaking the Waves*, London: Palgrave.

Pearce, L., 1997, *Feminism and the Politics of Reading*, London: Arnold, 1997.

Radway, J. A., 1991, *Reading the Romance: Women, Patriarchy and Popular Literature*, Chapel Hill: University of North Carolina Press.

Said, E., 1978, *Orientalism*, New York, Pantheon Press.

Slee, N., 2004, *Women's Faith Development: Patterns and Processes*, Aldershot: Ashgate.

Sharma, S., 2011, *Good Girls, Good Sex: Women Talk about Church and Sexuality*, Winnipeg: Fernwood Publishing

Schüssler Fiorenza, E., 1995, *Bread Not Stone: The Challenge of Feminist Biblical Interpretation*, Boston: Beacon Press.

Strhan, A., 2015, *Aliens and Strangers: The Struggle for Coherence in the Everyday Lives of Evangelicals*, Oxford: Oxford University Press.

Thistlethwaite, S., 1989,. *Sex, Race, and God*, London: Geoffrey Chapman.

Trzebiatowska, M., 2013, 'Beyond Compliance and Resistance: Polish Catholic Nuns Negotiating Femininity', *European Journal of Women's Studies*, Volume: 20 issue: 2: 204-218.

Walker, A., 1991 [1983], *The Color Purple*, Cambridge: Cambridge University Press.

Walton, H., 2007, *Literature, Theology and Feminism*, Manchester, Manchester University Press.

Walton, H., 2007, *Imagining Theology: Women, Writing and God*, London: T&T Clark.

Walton, H., 2008,'Our Sacred Texts: Literature, Theology and Feminism', in *Reading Spiritualities: Constructing and Representing the Sacred*, edited by D. Llewellyn and D.F. Sawyer, Aldershot: Ashgate: 85-98.

Talking Gender and Liberation

Towards a Generous Christian Social Ethic of Gender

GILL FRIGERIO

As believers work through the implications of their faith for their own ethical responses to the salient issues of our times, we each weave together lines of thought, our experiences and our prayerful consideration to construct our own stance. This is work no one can do for us. However much we read or debate there is not a ready made, off the shelf solution that will make total sense. Our own stance, as it is formed, can then be shared with others and contribute to their own thinking. This is particularly important if we have a perspective or experience that has been previously overlooked or excluded.

This article models a process of inner conversation to make explicit that process for one particular Christian woman, at the invitation of the editors. The article is structured as a dialogue, with questions and responses that might help you formulate your own stance, noting what resonates or jars for you. As well as showing the workings of an emerging theology, the dialogue draws on voices from a wide range of sources and seeks to deliberately cite women and writers of colour throughout.

Tell us a bit about yourself and your interest in this issue

I'm probably a cliché of what is sometimes referred to as 'white feminism' – British, middle-aged, middle class, straight married mother of two. I'm a lay Anglican, and not exactly a minority profile in the average Church setting. The other institutional space I regularly navigate is higher education, in my work as an Associate Professor in the Centre for Lifelong Learning at the University of Warwick.

I moved into higher education teaching having worked in Careers Advice for many years, and now I teach and supervise students who are working in career development alongside their studies. My own research considers the role of vocation and calling within working lives, bringing together secularised and theological understandings of calling. Within that, I am researching Christian women's experiences and perspectives as my starting point – a corrective to the typical pattern of knowledge creation of researching on and with men before considering whether things are different for women!

So my interest in gender issues is personal, as a woman, and professional. In my teaching I see gender as a key concept in career development. Only by exploring this will we start to understand why women's greatly increased participation in the workforce has not led to anything like equal access to the most powerful positions at the top of organisations, and why this does not seem to be simply a question of time.

Theologically, this leads me to integrate my own understanding of gender within the wider framework of my faith – how it sits alongside the rest of my beliefs, and beyond that what all those beliefs mean for how I live out my faith.

What does gender mean to you?

Firstly, to distinguish it from sex, it's not so much about my biology but is more about the way women and men move through and interact with social spaces. I find it helpful to think about my place in the world as linked systems, each with components which mutually influence one another. At an individual level my gender is part of my personhood along with my physical and psychological characteristics. Within my social contexts, all these components come together to interact with those around me, and on a grander scale, my position within the wider world at this time.

This means I am less interested in considering whether there are hard-wired sex differences such as women being better than men at multi-tasking but worse at reading maps. Gender is constructed rather than an outworking of essential sex differences which defines men and women as 'equal but different' and therefore best operating in complement to one another in fixed roles. Instead, men and women have learned to be different. The wider world, however, has been organised by men in positions of power in ways they consolidate that power – what we might call 'patriarchy'.

That word 'power' is significant here and is used in lots of ways besides gender, reflecting its unequal distribution and use in oppressions. We will come back to that later.

And how does that mean you see God?

Firstly, I'd reject any idea of God as male! As is often said, I hold God to be 'beyond gender'. However, in a patriarchal context the ways humanity has learned to use gender as we move through the world has led to systematic denial of the full humanity of women, codified through use of scripture and development of doctrine.

So I see it as a constant balance between emphasising common humanity, with both men and women made in the image of God, and recognising where full humanity has been denied to some, by others.

And scripture?

In considering scripture I find myself repeatedly returning to questions about who wrote the text and for whom it was written. I see any given narrative of an event is partial and offers the perspective of the narrator, just as any interpretation or translation is partial. The selection of accounts which were canonically endorsed was socially situated too. The texts we draw on today are loaded with the political and social context in which they were written. As we invite the Holy Spirit to speak to us today through them, this needs careful consideration.

Other texts can help us too. Reading the novel *The Wild Girl* by Michele Roberts at the age of 19, was pivotal for me in underlining my understanding of how standpoint determines what is left in and what is left out. The book offers a fictionalised account of power struggles in the early Church, particularly between Mary Magdalene and Peter, and the fuss that greeted Dan Brown's later novel *The Da Vinci Code* with its suggestion that a pregnant Mary Magdalene reached France, when Roberts depicted that twenty years earlier, shows how women's perspectives are so easily forgotten and lost.

I find it useful to bring forth the women who are named in scripture and inviting women to consider these stories alongside their own experience. Let's make sure we remember Anna as well as Simeon in the Lukan narrative of the presentation in the temple. Let's notice where women like Lydia, Dorcas and Phoebe are named and imaginatively consider their experiences. But we also need to reinterpret them. I find Schussler Fiorenza's (1984) fourfold hermeneutic of suspicion, remembrance, proclamation and actualisation helpful here. For example, take Martha and Mary. Martha is often presented as a woman juggling many domestic duties, taken for granted by the wider group. This in itself can be a powerful encounter, and I can certainly identify with it, but it remains problematic in both the writer's and then interpreters' spin on Jesus's response. Beginning with 'suspicion' we can realise the assumptions that have been made over time about Martha's role being domestic. In fact the word 'diakona' used for her 'service' could well refer to work outside the home. The doing/being dynamic represented by Mary and Martha can then be reconsidered in relation to ministry, or work in the public sphere.

And the Church?

Like many a social institution, I see the church as having worked into its DNA an unequal, dualistic theology of gender that depicts woman as embodied (as opposed to man as 'head'), sexual, powerless, instinctively caring and nurturing. This is why we have so many instances where women's ministry is denied or is under developed. In my own Church, we have traditionally higher attendance and participation of women than men, and roughly equal numbers now going forward to train for ministry. However, patterns relating to age and mode of training mean that women are unlikely to progress to the most influential positions or to lead the largest churches at the same rate as men. It is easy to point to this being a time limited problem: women have only been ordained as priests for 25 years and appointed as bishops for 5. However, the gendered theologies and patterns set in place through history and which have led to the current situation where those who do not accept women's priesthood as valid are still entitled to 'mutual flourishing' seem to me to point to a deeply embedded pattern that will need more transformative action to lead to real change.

So, you'd call yourself a feminist then?

I've no problem in calling myself a feminist and exploring feminist ideas to develop my thinking, praying and living. But it is a complex term. It is often defined as the pursuance of equality between men and women, but that seems under ambitious to me. A levelling up of women and men won't address other forms of inequality and oppression and I would argue for something more transformative.

Feminisms are diverse, too, and have evolved in 'waves'. Early waves such as the suffrage movement looked for women to participate in established structures. More radical forms of feminism see the oppression of women as fundamental, cutting across other forms associated with race and class and look for revolutionary responses. Material feminism focuses on the economic systems' oppressions, whereas cultural feminism is associated with generalisations about all women sharing gendered characteristics. We have feminisms that focus on individual freedoms and eco-feminism which links treatment of women with patriarchal dominance over the earth's resources.

Returning to the 'systems' idea I mentioned earlier, though, if we are all constructed through an interplay of individual and social components, then it stands to reasons that generalisations about women inherent in many of these feminisms must be open to challenge.

One principle challenge is that feminism centres the experiences of privileged, white, western women. That black women's experiences are not represented by feminism led to the development of the term 'womanist'. Alice Walker wrote 'Womanism is to feminism as purple is to lavender', and womanist thought is much more than 'black feminism', described by Wilda Gafney as a 'richer, deeper, liberative paradigm'.

A helpful way of considering these problems with feminisms is to look at how aspects of identity 'intersect'. Legal scholar Kimberle Crenshaw coined the term 'intersectionality' (Crenshaw, 1991) to convey some of this overlapping of forms of oppression. So, I'm probably most comfortable with the label 'intersectional feminist'.

What do you mean by 'intersectional'?

The intersection metaphor of road junctions on our path through life allows us to consider the unique circumstances of each individual, in context. With each individual's unique circumstances as central, this is then mediated through aspects of personal identity (changeable and unchangeable), then forms of discrimination such as racism, homophobia or sexism, which in turn are held in place by forces which compound and maintain that discrimination such as socio-economic structures, colonisation and globalisation. This is portrayed by the Canadian Research Institute for Advancement of Women (CRIAW/ICREF) wheel of intersectionality in fig 1 (Jayakumar, 2017).

So this calls into question how well different forms of feminism can handle the existence of other forms of oppression and acknowledge the diversity of women's experience. Clearly, women are not the only people who are disadvantaged by unequal social structures, lack of opportunity, discrimination, violence and the myriad ways that the status quo is maintained. Race, sexuality, class, disability and culture are just some of the other forms of oppression we need to consider. These intersect to compound disadvantage.

So what does being an intersectional feminist mean for you then?

What that means for my view of the world then is that is not simply *a patriarchy* (a dualistic system which represses across a number of axes and renders public space male). This is reflected in social structures and construct that limit power to a narrow demographic and has impact beyond gender: indeed Schussler Fiorenza's term 'kyriarchy' or 'rule of the master' reflects other forms of oppression. This in turn shows how the negative impact on women who have multiple disadvantages is greater.

The term 'master' particularly evokes colonial and white dominance over those of other races and particularly the legacy of oppressive regimes such as slavery. Feminism in its development has not until quite recently considered the intersection of race and gender but intersectionality reminds us of how they can compound one another. White women have been criticised for silencing black women within feminism, seeking to speak for all women. It is easy to fall into the trap of 'white feminism', in its worst forms this can look a lot like a middle class hobby, commodified into 'Girl power' sweatshirts.

So being an intersectional feminist reminds me that not all women are battling all forms of oppression and reminds me to 'check my privilege' that comes from being white, educated, cis-gendered, western, middle class, straight and able-bodied.

These same principles, that gender is a spectrum rather than a duality, and that not all women experience gender in the same way, can be useful in considering the particular issues for transgender women (women who were assigned male at birth). Recent years have seen increased public awareness of the particular issues for trans women and this has led to some debate about the compatibility of trans inclusion and the aims of feminism. For me, going back to the principles I outlined earlier I want to include trans women as women. Sure, I accept that a trans woman who was socialised as a boy would not have shared some of my formative experiences of girlhood. But neither have I had to negotiate the process of gender transition, and the evidence of suicide and violence for those who have suggests to me that I should be generous and welcoming.

This awareness of intersectionality at its worst can lead to what Roxanne Gay calls the 'Privilege and Oppression Olympics' and leads to difficult and highly charged exchanges. It is sad to see what Robin di Angelo terms 'white fragility' on display when feminists are asked to consider these issues. So one of my preoccupations is how we can become more comfortable having the necessary conversations to bring these tensions into the light. Hence my interest in plundering my own thought processes for this article.

How do you see gender and work?

As I explained, my professional life reflects my interests in women's' working lives and in gender and career development. I have my own experience as a woman with a working life and I also work with women as students, clients and colleagues as well as engaging with literature on women's working lives. So it's pertinent to comment on work in general and women's careers in particular.

Work is a key site for theological consideration representing economic forces of control and oppression as well as a space for agency, creativity and fulfilment. I recognise that the term 'career' has associations for many of particular types of working lives – those in high status occupations or with particular trajectories. I seek to use in a more inclusive way to represent the path through working life of all people.

There is much written about how careers develop, and this is the theoretical base for my professional practice. However, this knowledge is not complete: the career studies literature has been dominated by andro-centric explanations for understanding career decisions and trajectories, with an absence of women's voices and experiences

There have been recent efforts to address this and consider women's career development as an urgent priority given that increased educational attainment and participation in the workforce by women has not been matched by equality of status or pay, despite legislation. Women remain under represented in positions of power and gender pay gaps stubbornly persist. Women's work is highly vertically and horizontally segregated, focusing in a narrow range of roles, often with flexible conditions to facilitate caring and corresponding low pay/status and barriers to progression. Reasons and proposed solutions are varied, but often focus on women fixing things themselves, developing different aspirations or 'leaning in' to their ambition, as we were encouraged by Facebook Chief Operating Officer Sheryl Sandberg in her 2013 book.

Bringing the earlier consideration of gender and feminism to bear on women's career development, it is interesting to reflect on 'care' and work for women. The 'double duty' of responsibilities in the home and at work is a key feature of much discussion of why women might struggle to 'Lean In' to their working lives. When we are considering women and work Richardson and Schaeffer (2013) remind us to look at market work and unpaid care work and relationships in both domains and propose the framing question "How do women construct lives of meaning through work and relationship?" (Patton, 2013: 8). Women are co-constructing their lives through market work, unpaid care work, personal relationships and market work relationships and that consideration of women's working lives must explore and embrace all these dimensions.

I've already suggested that women are socialised as carers rather than having an innate ability to be better to both caring work (undervalued and underpaid) and unpaid familial caring. Women's career development is often framed as how can we get women (back) into the workplace and progressing their careers. There is a veneer of privilege about this – after all, being able to stay at home with children has been a luxury of the woman who does not need to earn. Lower down the social pecking order, women always worked, taking shifts and making shared childcare arrangements that enabled this whilst stuck in poor working conditions and unable to progress. For black women, this might have involved considerable family disruption and migration. Womanist theologians in the US point out that for many black women, work was looking after the children of white women rather than their own.

How does this relate to your own work in education?

One of the writers who has been influential for many in my field is Paulo Friere, who coined the idea of 'critical pedagogy' as a model of education with the potential to truly liberate and transform the wider social order. Friere (1968) shares liberation theology's preferential option for the poor and advocates for an educational stance that begins with the development of critical consciousness. His claims that humanity's vocation is to become more fully human and proposes a praxis (both action and reflection) of liberation as a process of humanisation.

Bringing this to my work, it means I have a general interest in work as liberating and transformative for all. This includes women of course, but if the goal of feminism is gender equality then its not going far enough. Equality assumes an alignment of women and men, yet intersectionality tells us also that not all men are equal. Further, equality denies the prophetic liberating power of the gospel to destabilise existing social order (Reuther, 1984) and usher in a new Earth for all. I have come to see equality as a staging post towards a more transformational reimagining of work, career and beyond. Equality with men ignores the impact of deficient theologies on men, and the restrictive masculinities available to them. Men also face barriers to life in all its fullness.

And what is your hope for the future?

From the threads I have woven together here, there are themes about how identity is form through mutual interaction and relationship, how binaries and dualisms create opposition and difference and how experience of others must be heard and respected. These themes of *relationality* and *mutuality* are often how feminist theologians conceptualise the Divine. This brings God amongst us, connecting us as interdependent and empowering us to be the image of God (Carter Heyward, 1989). For women this can be particularly empowering, seeing woman as source and norm rather than as 'other'.

Within this paradigm, Jesus models relationship and becomes brother and friend rather than objectifying instrument of patriarchy. Fran Porter's reimagining of gender relations in post-Christendom advocates a hermeneutic of friendship (2015), and I find this a valuable model in continuation of Jesus's inclusive community building and in order to avoid any sweeping assumptions about individual men. Fixed definitions of masculinity and femininity are problematic for all. Individual men therefore are affected by patriarchy and are not the enemy.

I think this leaves us in a strong position to develop a liberative social ethic as men and women. Friere distinguishes between activism (unreflective and futile) and action (a praxis combined with reflection). So I am keen to carve out spaces, for prayerful, collective reflection on gender and other forms of identity, as a necessary basis for transformative action.

Gill Frigerio is an Associate Professor in the Centre for Lifelong Learning at the University of Warwick.

Questions for discussion

1. What conversations do you need to have, with yourself and others, to work through your own stance on feminism and social ethics?

2. Where do you see power operating along the lines of gender, race and other intersecting identities in your daily life?

References

Carter Heyward, I. (1989) *Touching our Strength*. Brisbane: Harper Collins Australia

Crenshaw, K. W. (1991) *Mapping the margins: Intersectionality, identity politics, and violence against women of color*. Stanford Law Review 43 (6): 1241-1299

DiAngelo, R. (2018) *White Fragility: Why it's so hard for white people to talk about racism*. Boston, MA: Beacon Press.

Friere, P. (1968) *Pedagogy of the Oppressed*. New York: Continuum.

Gafney, W. (2017) *Womanist Midrash: A Reintroduction to the Women of the Torah and the Throne*. Louisville, KY: Westminster John Knox Press.

Gay, R. (2014) *Bad Feminist*. London: Corsair.

Jayakumar, K. (2017) *Understanding Intersectionality*. https://medium.com/the-red-elephant-foundation/understanding-intersectionality-a1da46e2e0b2 (accessed 26 January 2020)

Patton, W. (Ed.) *Conceptualising women's working lives: Moving the boundaries of discourse*. Rotterdam: Sense Publishers.

Porter, F. (2015) *Women and Men after Christendom*. Milton Keynes, Paternoster/Authentic Media Limited

Roberts, M. (1984) *The Wild Girl*. London: Methuen Modern Fiction.

Ruether, R.R. (1983) *Sexism and God-Talk: Toward a Feminist Theology*. Boston, MA: Beacon Press.

Sandberg, S. (2013) *Lean in: Women, work and the will to lead*. New York: Alfred A Knopf Inc.

Schussler Fiorenza, E. (1985) *Bread Not Stone: The Challenge of Feminist Biblical Interpretation*. Boston, MA: Beacon Press

Walker, A. (1984) *In Search of Our Mothers' Gardens: Womanist*. London: Women's Press

Further Reading

Reni Eddo Lodge. *Why I am no Longer Talking to White People about Race.*
Chimamanda Ngozi Adichie. *We Should all be Feminists.*

Forum

A History of Brexit: A Review Essay

Matt Bullimore

After Brexit? European Unity and the Unity of European Churches
Mattias Grebe and Jeremy Worthen, eds.
Evangelische Verlagsanstalt, 2019, 157pp., pbk, £27.08

Theologising Brexit: A Liberationist and Postcolonial Critique
Anthony G. Reddie
Routledge, 2019, x + 255pp., hbk, £120.00

It already seems like a lot of history has happened since the Referendum was held on 23 June 2016 to decide whether Britain would leave the European Union. We would be unwise to think that it is all behind us, even though the Prime Minister signed the Withdrawal Agreement on 24 January 2020. The subsequent negotiations and discussions will no doubt prove to be eventful. The last (nearly) four years have given some time to reflect on how we have ended up where we are whilst we have been watching the drama of the 'how' we will leave play out. As these two books being reviewed here show, the history behind the Referendum is much longer than recent, if interminable, current affairs. For one, it is a history that stretches back to the age of Empire, colonialism and slavery. For the other, modern Europe – its nations and its churches – cannot be understood without going back at least as far as the end of the Second World War.

There are multiple histories that lie behind what we cannot avoid calling Brexit. Although it is a political decision with economic ramifications, it also has social causes and consequences. Brexit has become a whole cultural phenomenon. Indeed, the very name itself now feels like some incantation that conjures, depending on your feelings about the matter, a demon or an angel with respective armies of Remainers or Leavers. The binary logic of the Referendum has brought with it real and stark divisions that have begun to define the zeitgeist despite the subtleties of every aspect of what Brexit means and stands for. It is the complexity of the phenomenon that requires in-depth analyses. These two books consider those things that were considered germane as people voted but, perhaps more importantly, also what was obscured or forgotten. Both books look at the causes of and motivations behind our decisions and offer some prospect of what now needs to be done.

Despite unearthing histories – both overt and hidden – underlying the discourses around Brexit, the books are very different. *Theologising Brexit* (TB) is the less sanguine. Anthony G. Reddie identifies an ignorance at the heart of contemporary theological and ecclesiastical responses to Brexit and foregrounds the plight of Black people and communities in the UK. In fact, as Reddie acknowledges, his is not a book about the EU and the benefits/disadvantages of the EU project or its current organization. It is a book about that which still remains unconscious, hidden or ignored and yet remains hugely formative of who and how we are. It is a book about White privilege, and about White privilege as something which is a problem both for peoples of colour and for White people. Reddie looks behind Brexit and finds what is for him a familiar enemy and one which is so unduly successful because still so unacknowledged.

After Brexit? (AB) is framed more positively. It finds that there are seeds of hope in the way that the European Union was formed and in the way European churches have worked together. The churches embedded in Europe could still have a transformational social impact whether the UK is within or without the EU. It contains discussions of the impetus for the founding of the EU project and the contribution of the churches, as well as analyses of the pattern of social divisions across Europe and the place of Christianity in European culture. There are also essays that reflect theologically on what the churches might need to do to witness to the Good News in this area of the world.

Both books are concerned with the Church's voice, therefore. Who does that voice represent? How is that voice heard? What has that voice obscured? How has that voice been effective in the past? Who is left without voice or agency? Whom can that voice enfold? What needs to be said and what needs to be heard, and by whom? For one, history discloses injustices that recur and abide, and for the other there is a history that discloses a serious Christian witness embedded in political institutions and economic agreements. They are histories that exert a pressure on the present but both volumes agree that history will neither finally save nor damn us, but what we do now will.

The common threads throughout diverse essay topics in Reddie's book are Black Christianity, Whiteness and Empire. They witness to a toxic mix of Christianity, Colonialism and Racism, which he sees as fundamental to White identity and which has shaped Black bodies and minds and defined how communities experience belonging in the UK. The relentlessness of the critique is uncomfortable but before questions are posed of the analyses or of any claims or omissions, the book requires that the reader stop and attend. It is drawing out something which is for the most part unconscious and that we are not used to hearing. Before any ifs and buts, we have to participate in the labour of allowing what he is arguing to manifest itself in our hearts and minds. We need to hear what he has to say.

Note well that it is a book addressed to Black and White alike. Reddie is frustrated by the Black votes for Brexit. They were, he contends, votes for a romanticized version of Christian Britain that were ignorant of the way that the inevitable social divisions would impact on Black lives in the UK. More painfully still, perhaps, Reddie describes an internalized colonization and self-negation in Black minds and Black churches which continues to sap Black communities of agency and hinders the possibility of critical reflection and positive action. The book discerns the need for a common project of the deconstruction of that toxic mix that underlies both White treatment of the Other and also the self-understanding of minority Black cultures as they negotiate a life in Britain.

There is always a need for intersectional thinking. How do discourses around class and gender overlap and mix together? A Marxist analysis will often ask, rightly, what part class plays in racist discourses. There is ample work on this (eg, David Roediger). But there is also the need to attend to specific areas of disadvantage and oppression which remind us not to reduce systems of oppression to any one master analysis but to consider each in their specificity as well as their intersection. Perhaps Reddie's book does not attend in detail to many of the wider class issues around Brexit but he reminds us that White economic disadvantage is, when all is said and done, White. To be White is still normal, usual. There is a fragile blend of entitlement, exceptionalism and superiority that needs to be broken where it manifests. And it has at times manifested itself around Brexit even if we might also want to ask what common cause there is between economic underclasses.

If *Theologising Brexit* does not dwell on either Brexit itself or the EU, neither is it systematically theological. He describes how Black theology operates by way of a series of essays that foreground its alliance with critical and sociological analyses. Black theology is a tool for critically reading the signs of the times in a post-Truth world. Black theology is for him is a prophetic liberation theology. It recovers and brings together subterranean traditions that might help build a non-colonial and more humane Church. There is a tension in Reddie's book between the way Black theology operates in liberative mode and the blackness of the Church. We hear that blackness is always in crisis. Its theology therefore is always critical, prophetic, subversive, deconstructive. It seeks liberation and offers critique. In that sense it is a negative theology, struggling against dominant discourses. Would Black theology come to an end as a discipline if it saw the hoped-for liberation and successfully subverted White discourses, we might ask? On the other hand, Reddie gestures towards that which is constructive, positive and substantive in Black theology. Writing of the Windrush generation, he describes a theology which is generous, convivial and faithful. It is hospitable, open to the Other and personalist. We also hear of multicultural optics that refuse the monoculture of White supremacy, of a being at home with hybridity, and of a spirituality drawn from cultures African, Caribbean, Rastifarian, Christian. In fact, this is a new theological anthropology that is ideally suited for a Pilgrim people able to belong in multiple ways. An anthropology that, I hope, could be a gift of Black Christians to the Church that it might be more Black.

Reddie hopes for a greater agency for white people. He calls this the labour of a practical theological anthropology. He wants to set all people free from Whiteness. He wants them to learn how to cede their privilege in order to thrive. How can we be Christ unless we are able to identify with Christ's own solidarity with the poor as one marginalized and reviled? Pedagogy, as those familiar with Reddie's work will know, is a key part of this liberating labour. He advocates a participative Black theology that inspires ordinary people to radical social change. It aims at a conscientization that uses encounter to engage the whole range of affective, imaginative and rational faculties of people in order to expand their world and offer new ways of knowing, living and being.

There will no doubt continue to be the need for a certain communitarianism that enables Black people to learn and embed what he calls a Black phronesis. It is a practical wisdom learnt in traditioned communities and there is still the necessity of mutual support and strengthening in an environment that is threatening and oppressive. It comes, of course, with a danger of isolation and division. It is therefore the glimpse of the Kingdom in its Blackness for all people – the eschatological perspective – that I would invite Reddie to articulate further, because it is a tool in helping us to forswear our Whiteness. It shows us why we cannot be ourselves as the Church until we have understood that we need to welcome humbly the gift of one another. The task of the White is to do better. To be better. And our plea should be: Friend, continue to teach me, and be Christ to me, so I can learn to be Christ to you.

The focus of *After Brexit?* is quite different. It investigates the changing nature of European unity and the implications this has for the unity of the European churches. It asks what the unity of the churches, by way of response, might have to say to those who seek a way forward for the political, social and cultural unity of Europe. The contributors are well aware that the EU is not Europe and some of the more engaging chapters describe the way that the EU itself came into being and the Christian social teachings that undergirded its foundation. The book is the product of a colloquium in late 2018 at Lambeth that was hosted by the Archbishop of Canterbury and his guest, the Chair of the Evangelische Kirche in Deutschland.

The first section of the book is historical. By understanding the part played by the churches at the beginning of the EU project and their subsequent contributions to European culture we will have more of a sense of what part they can and need to play now. There are fascinating contributions by Piers Ludlow and Gary Wilton on Robert Schuman and his fellow architects of the EU and their solidly Christian – if silent – witness. A blend of political Catholicism, alive to Catholic Social Teaching, and more Protestant Christian democracy undergirded this initially economic settlement that sought to avoid any relapse into conflict. The former would come to stress what was common whilst the latter would stress the national (eg, Great Britain, Scandinavia) in subsequent negotiations. But by placing coal and steel under a common Authority it brought about economic solidarity, mutual interdependence and distributed control of the means of waging war. The project was federalist, not wanting to weaken nation states, but rather to strengthen them through commonality. The specifically Christian principles that inspired this tension between the particular and the common were, however, unacknowledged as such. Memories of conflicts gravitating around confessional identities in Europe are obstinate.

The authors of AB bring out some of the questions that this leaves us with today. Is confessional language so offensive in the public square today or are we postsecular enough to acknowledge that a healthy pluralism is found where all agencies are able to share and shape public space? Or is religion increasingly irrelevant to most people? How does Europe cope with the loss of its obvious external threat – the Communist bloc – and what happens when the key threat has been linked to the growing and ethnically diverse communities which make up European public space and which continue to migrate towards prosperity? What happens when religion is co-opted by Nationalist and Populist right-wing movements and can the Church offer a truer Christianity that welcomes the humanity of every Other? Indeed, is it possible for the churches to be involved in the promotion of a European culture that is not defined by threat, issues of sovereignty or economic interest? It may well be, as Bishop Nick Baines is quoted as arguing, that this is a more necessary task today given that the postwar narratives of peace-as-integration are losing traction as the drivers of European unity.

The book's second section looks more closely at European society and the place of the churches within it today. Toxic social divisions, exacerbated by the consequences of economic globalization, demand theological responses. There is a need to articulate, as at the inception of the EU, the way the national and the international, the local and the universal, the distinctive and the common can be mediated. Interestingly, as for Reddie, the term hybridity emerges as something peculiar to a Pilgrim people who are located in the here and now but of another City.

Ben Ryan investigates practical church solutions for societies that manifest an increasingly fractured and polarized public arena. He looks at tensions between Anywheres and Somewheres, between the metropolitan and liberal socially-agile and those in often challenging but cohesive communities, and examines the inter-generational strife that exacerbates those tensions. He looks in particular at the face off between Christianism (a cultural position defined negatively against

Forum

the Other – usually Islam) and Christianity as a faith that loves the neighbour. He sets out a programme of practical action on three levels – the local where community organizing brings people together in common cause, the intermediate role of churches in advocacy for the marginalized, and the more national role of articulating a vision and the values that contribute to a plural but common public space. He concludes by reminding us that belonging can be about both rational choice and also be a more affective phenomenon that relies on feeling that we have agency, power to participate and stable identities. Arnulf von Scheliha and Grace Davie offer Protestant and Anglican analyses, respectively, of European society, its divisions and the prospects for the churches' present and future role in promoting tolerance and freedom and by contributing still to the shape and tone of institutional structures.

The third section digs deeper into the response of the churches to the changes in European society. Bishop Sarah Rowland Jones offers a theologically rich account of the Church as the Body of Christ witnessing to what human co-belonging is really all about. She writes knowing the bishops in Wales – as indeed, England – believed themselves to be speaking for the poor by advocating Remain and yet were ignorant of the way that many people felt that their interests were not recognized in public discourse and so voted Leave. We might note that this is a problem not just for the Church but the for the Left in general, where the desire to stand in solidarity with the marginalized meant a celebration of the referendum result even where this seemed to stand in opposition to what many Leftist analyses saw as the economic benefits of remaining. Rowland Jones offers Biblical insights into relational and humane Christian living whilst also being pragmatic and realistic about the ways people, and the institutions to which they cling, sin and fail. Hers is a nuanced and wise example of an ecclesiologically resonant social theology.

Will Adam, Matthias Grebe and Jeremy Worthen examine the ways in which European ecumenism has been conducted and how it might proceed. They note that institutional recounting of historical narratives of disunity and ecumenical progress may not be enough and that visible unity in the present will look more like common action across national borders. The collection is then brought to a conclusion by Archbishop Justin Welby who summarizes much of the discussion by emphasizing the radicality of Christian community and Christian virtues that stand out as distinctive in an often vicious political environment. He underlines our need to hold onto hope and to drive out fear together, and that unity is achieved when we embrace humility and seek forgiveness.

Both TB and AB demonstrate the complexity of the Brexit phenomenon with all of its political, cultural and social facets. Reddie focuses on Race, of which we hear less in AB. The latter volume is concerned instead with the ways in which the institutional churches have a part to play in the future of European society. What they both offer are depth analyses that point to histories of human being that exert their pressure on national, local and individual psyches. What they both contend is that theology has a crucial and necessary role in extolling the truly human amidst the changes in our social and political world which are often dehumanizing and dangerous. Both point to the fact that our analyses must be subtle and our actions demonstrative.

Matt Bullimore, Churchill College, Cambridge

Book Reviews

Reimagining Theologies of Marriage in Contexts of Domestic Violence: When Salvation is Survival
Rachel Starr
Routledge, 2018, xi + 225 pp., hbk, £105

Many Christian theological treatments of marriage have held that it is a phenomenon which promotes the goods of those in it: a secure foundation for the nurture of children and, indeed, the stability of society as a whole. Such theologies too infrequently acknowledge the ways in which marriages, and families founded on them, can be dangerous institutions, reinforcing norms of power and hierarchy and leaving some of their members (usually women and children) at the mercy of others (usually men, disproportionately the perpetrators of domestic violence).

This book is different. Based in part on Starr's doctoral fieldwork in Argentina, it brings sociological, pastoral, and practical-theological literature into sensitively curated conversation, and engages with a range of Christian denominations' own work on intimate partner violence. Starr begins with the always sobering statistic that women are most at risk of abuse from the men in their own families and homes, and that a third of women in Argentina and a quarter in England and Wales experience domestic violence during their lifetimes. She holds that, in both contexts, Christian beliefs, teachings and practices about marriage are 'risk factors'.

For example, in Argentina in particular, the figure of Mary the mother of Jesus is held up as an ideal of female submission and obedience, sometimes used to discourage women from challenging their circumstances. Theologically inflected assumptions that women should not have control over their own reproductive decision-making (with regard, for example, to contraception or termination of pregnancy) tend to undermine women's agency, and this is important not least because domestic violence happens to many women for the first time during pregnancy. Comparing ideals and realities of marriage shows powerfully that theologians' appeals to marriage and family life as positive and even as salvific requires problematization.

Indeed, Starr notes that some Christian denominations have begun this work, pointing to attempts by the Methodist Church in Britain and the Church of England to dismantle hierarchical accounts of gender and push back at theologies based on redemptive violence. Yet, she argues, "Long-established notions of marriage and marital roles still need to be reassessed. If not, mainstream churches will continue to denounce only what is regarded as extraordinary physical violence, without tackling the underlying symbolic inequalities present within many theologies of marriage" (p.43).

In particular, Starr examines covenantal and sacramental models of marriage and their impacts on domestic violence. In both cases she notes that such models *can* be very egalitarian and empowering for women, but that aspects of them remain freighted. For example, the covenantal model seems to reinforce notions of symbolic super-ordination and subordination that map onto human gendered spousal relationships. Where fidelity is understood solely or mainly in terms of sexual exclusivity, there may be too little acknowledgement of how violence itself comprises lack of faith. Similarly, viewing marriage as sacrament *can* render it a place for the exercise of self-sacrificial love. However, too often this has meant costly sacrifice by wives and children; especially when sacramentality has been equated with indissolubility and so women have been discouraged by their church leaders from leaving abusive marriages. Rather, insists Starr, 'In contexts of domestic violence, neither sacrifice nor suffering can be understood as redemptive' (148), and women must seek first to preserve their own and their children's safety.

Starr's detractors might retort that marriage which becomes a setting for violence and abuse is not marriage as God intended it to be, and that the fact so many marriages are bad ones does not in itself undermine the goodness of marriage in principle. Yet one might hold in response that we know marriage only via actual *marriages*, and that there are plenty of instances where churches (among other bodies) have seemed to render marriage *per se* morally immaculate without caring to interrogate what goes on behind closed doors. As Starr says mildly: 'Problems occur when churches fail to acknowledge the gap between the ideal and reality' (81).

Starr holds that churches' complicity with domestic abusers, whether explicitly or simply by failing to act to protect victims when abuse is brought to their attention, is an outworking of structural sin. Churches must interrogate their own collusion with violence, and reject the notion that intimate partner and familial abuse are private matters. Churches should engage in the 'saving work' of deconstructing male domination, vocally denouncing violence, and offering practical and spiritual support to survivors.

There is much in this clear, accomplished book with the potential to challenge and convict. Starr is always measured, and does not stray into rhetoric despite her sometimes harrowing subject matter. The brevity of her final chapter (on salvation as survival) is tantalising, and I hope the discussion will prompt further work.

Susannah Cornwall, University of Exeter

Undoing Theology: Life Stories from Non-Normative Christians

Chris Greenough,
SCM Press, 2018, ix + 219 pp., hbk, £65

Undoing Theology takes its title from a dialogue with Judith Butler's *Undoing Gender* in which she calls for the undoing of gender that is necessary before we can do ourselves. This undoing is dependent upon connection with and vulnerability to the other. Chris Greenough takes this task of undoing into the theological realm as he seeks to bring sexual stories into dialogue with theologies in order than theology might be undone by the reality, intimacy, and potency of the sexual stories we can tell.

The telling of sexual stories is a trope Greenough takes from the late Marcella Althaus-Reid. Greenough takes the reader through Althaus-Reid's sexual theology in the first part of this monograph, in a chapter that reads like a love letter to Althaus-Reid. Although not naïve to the limits of her work, it is clear that Greenough has been profoundly shaped in his approach to theology and theological methods by her approach to sexual theologies. Greenough takes Althaus-Reid's conviction that sexual storytelling is a catalyst for theology to heart as he approaches this task of undoing theology from the perspective of the sexual stories of non-normative Christians. He notes 'the in-depth, subjective, sexual stories Althaus-Reid calls for are lacking in her own work and have not been adequately addressed in academic terms by other theologians' (13). It is this gap that his monograph seeks to fill and begins to do so admirably.

Greenough engages with three narratives from non-normative Christians in the central three chapters of this volume; Alyce, an intersex woman who inhabits the body of a 62 year old man; Caddyman, an ex-gay survivor; and Cath, a woman who engages in 'polykinkerous,' non-sexual, BDSM. In each chapter, Greenough skilfully interweaves their narratives (told in their own words), with extensive engagement with the range of theological and sociological research surrounding particular issues (intersex, gay treatments, masculine spirituality and faith development, women's spiritualities, theological anthropologies to name just a few). Alongside this, Greenough constructs theology. He uses the sexual stories offered to us to undo traditional theological ideas and heteronormative theological assumptions to present a vision of theologies that are inclusive, real, and potent. Greenough draws these narratives and his theological constructions together in the final chapter as he argues that 'the task for theology is to undo dominant repetitions of Christian tradition in relation to gender, sexuality, and sex in order to make it more inclusive. Moreover, *undoing theology* uncovers the temporal nature of all theologies and life events.' (158, italics original).

Greenough is remarkably successful in demonstrating not only the necessity of telling such stories (and the gap that the lack of such stories presents in theological discourse) but in telling them, or rather in providing the space for them to be told. He presents these stories with sensitivity and a theologically critical eye that allows such narratives to become the space for a theological construction whilst always attending to the instability of experience as a theological source. Ultimately, he is able to reshape the contextual expectations about God and to creatively unbind God from these expectations as he releases (or at least begins to release) theology from heteronormative, chaste, un-real expectations.

If I have any criticism of this text, it is simply that I wanted Greenough to go much further than he did. Perhaps indicative of its origins as a PhD thesis that must cover its back at every turn, I wonder if Greenough's reflection on the precarity of experiential knowledge has made him a little too hesitant in claiming the ground available before him. Whilst he does an excellent job of weaving together story, research, and theological implication, there is space to claim much

Book Reviews

more ground. The chapter on BDSM particularly edged around some of the profound theological claims that could be made about the nature of spiritual experience, mystical union with the divine, and BDSM as theological method. I, for one, would be very keen to see this developed further as a relatively unmined source of theological reflection. However, this critique is a minor one merely reflecting a desire to hear more from this creative and innovative theologian.

I recommend this text to undergraduates and non-academic readers as an excellent introduction to sexual theologies. Greenough manages a comprehensive and yet very readable account of the attendant literature and research in this area that will surely be very valuable to those encountering this topic for the first time. Furthermore, for the graduate theologian, Greenough's monograph will surely be resource for teaching as well as challenge to, in the grand tradition of Althaus-Reid, do our theologies with our knickers off; a provocation as to the exciting results such theological endeavour could produce.

Karen O'Donnell, Sarum College

The Character Gap: How Good are We?

Christian B. Miller
Oxford University Press, 2018, xvii + 276 pp., hbk, £15.17

This short, conversational text aims to explore largely philosophical and briefly theological accounts of morality. It does so through a particular lens, that of character, and character as it pertains to assessing humans as moral agents. It is a book intended to appeal to a wide audience and situates itself thus: whilst Aristotle's account of the virtues and Kant's ethics underpin the work; they are presented as one of many philosophical accounts of the virtues. The focus is instead on what social psychological reveals about our character, rather than philosophical argumentation. This is then augmented with a brief exposition of a Christian understanding of virtue at the end of the book.

The book thus wants to cover a lot of ground and quite quickly. There is thus an emphasis on breadth rather than depth, such as in the first two chapters on character. Here the book hones in on character as formed by either practising virtues or vices. However, the book wants to posit not that are, by nature, good people nor that we are especially bad people (with some notable exceptions). Instead, the vast majority of us are good at times, bad at other times, and this must spill over into our view of humanity. Miller sees that most of the time we associate or describe as friends people who we see as virtuous, or if not so overall, at least in some ways. But, for Miller, this entails that people who we do not see as worthy of friendship, or people across political divides are seen as less virtuous, or as having worse characters than our friends. There is a stress initially here on self-examination, that there is a gap between how we perceive ourselves (generally good) and how we actually are (middling at best). This is the character gap and Miller seeks to show that 'most people do not in fact have any virtues, and most people do not in fact have any vices' (20). This work is drawn from more detailed work that Miller has been engaged in on this topic, and thus this book aims to be a more accessible (to non-academics and subject specialists) account of his research.

To illustrate and ground this assessment of humanity, Miller turns to a variety of social psychological experiments on character, morality, and how people act and how they are influenced to act. Some of these are renowned, such as the Milgram experiments in which the participants were prepared to, and often did, administer a fatal electric shock to someone when instructed to by an authority figure even if reluctant and initially unwilling. Despite this experiment, Miller sees that we are not by nature cruel. With recourse to a number of other experiments which claim to have gathered data on our propensity and capacity to help people; our ability and capability to harm people; and how, why, and how often we lie and cheat; Miller concludes from that evidence that whilst we are all capable of these actions, and with instantiations of the virtues and vices around them, we are not either virtuous or vicious. We are a mixture of the two, and one more at particular times and in particular contexts. This he sees as the psychological picture, and going forward Miller is deeply reliant on this, despite the fact (acknowledged by him in the final chapter) that correlation is not causation.

Miller then details strategies to explicitly make our character if not completely virtuous, as Aristotle would want it in the unity of the virtues, more virtuous, all of which have various shortcomings. Doing nothing is largely discounted, labelling ourselves as virtuous and having that influence our actions is another, less defeatist approach, as is setting up situations where we are nudged towards being virtuous. The use of moral role models, selecting situations in which we avoid vice and incline towards virtue, as well as the aforementioned call to self-examination of our desires. The book ends with an exploration of Christianity and the how it understands character and morality, and if one is religious, how to be more virtuous within that framework.

The topic of morality is a particularly large topic. It is a particularly contested topic, and both the approach (using social psychology) and the framework (largely virtue ethics with some deontology) are not necessarily universally accepted philosophically, and I did find that the reliance on these studies limited the work. The final chapters on what to do about this seemed to be hastily argued compared to how drawn out the evidencing was. This is perhaps inevitable considering it is based on more complex work and argumentation. And whilst this will not solve any moral crises, it will go some way towards helping people reconsider their own character and actions.

Deborah Casewell, Liverpool Hope University

Rethinking Holiness: A Theological Introduction
Bernie A. Van De Walle,
Baker Academic, 2018, xvi + 176 pp., pbk, £13.99

Van De Walle opens this book with two observations. On the one hand, 'holiness' is 'out of fashion' among evangelicals and others who count the late nineteenth-century Holiness movements as a valuable part of their heritage (xi). On the other hand, 'there is a widespread hunger for knowledge and experience of holiness' (xii), a phenomenon he details throughout chapter 1. But rather than offering an inconsistent narrative, Van De Walle has diagnosed something like a supply-and-demand problem: many people within and without the (evangelical) church are searching for holiness, but all it has to offer them is a practical morality, without any rich theological sense of what holiness is beyond a code of conduct. The book aims to address this problem by providing a richer theological account of holiness than is readily accessible within current evangelical thought and which is accessible on a popular level.

At heart, holiness is 'the transcendent or absolute otherness that is basic to God's being' (xiii). Its moral significance can only be rightly understood and enacted when this theocentric understanding of holiness is recognised. Van De Walle hopes that by the end of the book his reader understands holiness as a 'way of being' rather than a state one achieves by partaking in or abstaining from particular moral actions. This way of being is fundamentally devotional and the book frequently reflects this in its tone. In my view, he articulates the dynamic relationship between faith and ethics in holiness' most clearly in an aside contrasting his view with Donatism. He says 'For Donatists, holiness was about behaviour, full stop. But …while moral purity is something after which the church is to strive, the church's holiness refers more fundamentally to its relationship with and dependence on God' (144).

In order to convey his theology of holiness, Van De Walle structures his book clearly and consistently. Each chapter opens with an anecdote, conversationally covers the topic at hand and then closes with an excursus on a relevant difficult issue (framed historically or theologically). For instance, he addresses how an overemphasis on moral purity can become heretical, and how he sees political correctness and tolerance interfacing with questions of holiness.

The progression of chapters begins with evidencing the desire for holiness which the author sees in contemporary society (chapter 1). From there, he spends two chapters developing his theology of holiness, first from scriptural foundations (chapter 2) and second drawing on the Christian tradition (chapter 3). Because Chapter 3 essentially presents a doctrine of God, it and the subsequent chapters could almost serve as a systematic theology in miniature, treating major loci through the lens of holiness (understood as transcendence and moral purity). He covers anthropology (chapter 4), sin (chapter 5), salvation (chapter 6), and ecclesiology (chapter 7). If the reader is new to theological writings and from the same tradition as the author, this will provide them with a rudimentary foundation not only in a theology of holiness but also in basic theological categories, how they relate to one another, and what impact each has on practical considerations. This gives the book broader pedagogical applications than merely its titular topic. Within its denominational context, it could be an effective non-academic introduction to theology in general, as well as holiness in particular.

I emphasise Van De Walle's rootedness in the evangelical and North American holiness tradition because, his occasional use of patristic and medieval sources notwithstanding, there is no attempt to engage a broader audience or explicitly draw upon contemporary theology from beyond his tradition (though appeals to sanctification and participation may make some see an unspoken influence).

Book Reviews

Nevertheless, the theology he outlines does allow for and encourage such dialogue, and so should be seen has having a specific target audience rather than being an insular text.

There are at least two points where greater engagement with theologians of other traditions might have benefited his proposal. First, his treatment of divine transcendence rightfully emphases God's otherness and categorical distinction from created things, but it omits the important corollary of God's immanence; that God's unparalleled otherness means that God is also incomparably close to all God's creatures. The result is that 'transcendence' becomes a fancy word for saying 'distinctiveness' or a less fancy word for God's 'aseity.' There are times when he wishes to emphasise that what is holy may yet be present in the world (e.g. the church may be holy without self-imposed cultural isolation); at this and similar points, his omission of the divine immanence which is co-existent with divine transcendence does not serve him well. Conflates

Secondly, he conflates the intrinsic nature of qualities with the independent possession of such qualities. This is clear when he says that human holiness is never intrinsic because it is always dependent upon God, rather than something one has independently. The result is a sort of nominalism of holiness, where holiness is only that which is declared as such (a position he argues against later on). If Van De Ware acknowledged that a trait may be both intrinsic and dependent, he would not have this problem (e.g. human existence is dependent upon God at all times, and yet existence is intrinsic to what it is to be human).

Of course, most of Van De Ware's intended audience will not be reading at this level, and so such imprecisions may be excused. His book is meant to open minds to a new way of thinking, about holiness and theology, and from this entry point the reader is well set to find other sources to further augment and expand theologically-informed faithfulness.

E. S. Kempson, St Mellitus College.

Book Reviews

Christ and the Common Good: Political Theology and the Case for Democracy

Luke Bretherton
Eerdmans, 2019, viii + 522 pp., hbk, £34

Christ and the Common Good is a big book: ambitious in the scale of its argument, wide-ranging in its selected topics, and profound in its analyses and argument for democracy. As such, it is probably more than one book and could be read selectively as either a primer in political theology, or a political theology of a common life, or an articulation and defence of democratic politics as a Christian option. Its chief theological innovation is a stress on the significance of pneumatology to political theology. If the two dominant options in political theology are Christological-sacramental and Christological-eschatological, Bretherton seeks to add a third, pneumatology: a political theology of 'the second difference'. As such, the book is loosely organised, and tends to avoid the lure of binaries and the lurid discourse of the apocalyptic and offers instead an irenic tone and a flexible, mediating approach. Covering topics not often engaged in political theology (humanitarianism, Pentecostalism, for example) and thereby seeking to move political theology closer to practice, the book represents a very impressive achievement.

The bookend chapters indicate the arc of the argument. For theology, politics cannot be avoided, and theology is always in some way political; democratic politics is a valid way of doing politics and has theological warrant. As such, this book may qualify as an activist's theology: given the non-eliminability of political agency, what is the Christian task? In the making of this argument, the five case studies of part one could probably be skipped by the reader in a hurry, although each of them are fascinating. Indeed, the book's three parts are only loosely linked and no sustained conceptuality organises the whole book. Despite the book's title, the argument is not governed by a detailed Christology, and there is a recurring caution regarding concepts of order that accompany Christology. Some terms do recur: pneumatology from chapter 4 and 'consociational' from chapter 6 are picked up in subsequent parts. Yet the book could well be read as two books: a presentation of political theology (part 1), and a more constructive political theology (parts 2 and 3, on sustaining and forming a common life) for a European-North American context. Perhaps such multiple readings also raise the question of sequence:

Book Reviews

why does sustaining a common life precede forming a common life? This might be an outcome of the priority that Bretherton gives to pneumatology but it does leave the final chapter of the book, on democratic politics, removed from issues of communion, secularity and hospitality which are the central themes of part 2.

Those who are already familiar with Bretherton's writings will know that his work is closer to O'Donovan than Milbank, and closer to Hauerwas than Gutiérrez. Yet, *Christ and the Common Life* is a sustained effort to engage with a range of theologies in a generous spirit. Thereby matters of political theology are to be found in unlikely places. For example, the extended discussion of Black Power (not black theology) where the reader is invited to learn from the effort to create 'a nation within a nation'. Sometimes I wonder if in this blizzard of connections, yet more connections might be made: is not some effort to construct a group within a wider group also on offer in Latin American liberation theology, western Marxism, and some parts of postcolonial theology? I, for one, appreciate that the opening discussion on the nature of political theology is not framed by the work of Carl Schmitt, resisting a common approach that sees political theology beginning with Schmitt and as best understood in Schmittian perspective, which in turn enables a more hospitable construal of political theology. The absence of a Schmittian framing also means that the account of sovereignty that is presented in the final quarter of the book both provides a theological lineage and a more distributed account of authority. A range of political theologies present in Pentecostalism are also carefully presented: this is a much more sympathetic, and interesting, discussion of Pentecostalism than the usual obligatory reference to prosperity and elevation.

Strangely, the shortest chapter is the concluding chapter on democratic politics: democratic politics is 'the negotiation of a common life', but it is not clear what political theology adds to an account of such a negotiation. It is clear that the worshipping congregation marks a sort of boundary to politics (451). Perhaps this is the culmination of the anti-Schmittian stance of this enquiry: democratic politics functions in this argument as a practice and a location of agency and not as a set of ideas, although of course there are plenty of ideas to be had about such practices. Yet the reader is left in a difficult position having been instructed that people come before programme: after all, are there occasions when people do not come first (emergency times, to be sure) and what are those occasions and how are we to act in them? It is a question that any revolution must face, and it is a question to be faced when, as now, we live in a global emergency.

Peter Manley Scott, University of Manchester

The Canterbury Dictionary of HYMNOLOGY

The result of over ten years of research by an international team of editors, The Canterbury Dictionary of Hymnology is the major online reference work on hymns, hymn-writers and traditions.

www.hymnology.co.uk

CHURCH TIMES

The Church Times, founded in 1863, has become the world's leading Anglican newspaper. It offers professional reporting of UK and international church news, in-depth features on faith, arts and culture, wide-ranging comment and all the latest clergy jobs. Available in print and online.

www.churchtimes.co.uk

Crucible

Crucible is the Christian journal of social ethics. It is produced quarterly, pulling together some of the best practitioners, thinkers, and theologians in the field. Each issue reflects theologically on a key theme of political, social, cultural, or environmental significance.

www.cruciblejournal.co.uk

JLS

Joint Liturgical Studies offers a valuable contribution to the study of liturgy. Each issue considers a particular aspect of liturgical development, such as the origins of the Roman rite, Anglican Orders, welcoming the Baptised, and Anglican Missals.

www.jointliturgicalstudies.co.uk

magnet

Magnet is a resource magazine published three times a year. Packed with ideas for worship, inspiring artwork and stories of faith and justice from around the world.

www.ourmagnet.co.uk

For more information on these publications visit the websites listed above or contact **Hymns Ancient & Modern:**
Tel.: +44 (0)1603 785 910
**Write to: Subscriptions, Hymns Ancient & Modern,
13a Hellesdon Park Road, Norwich NR6 5DR**

CHEQUE OR CREDIT CARD	DIRECT DEBIT
Individual rate UK: ☐ £22	☐ £20
Institutional rate UK: ☐ £30	☐ £28
International rate: ☐ £40	☐ £35
Individual copy ☐ £7	

Crucible

Please complete section 1. Cheque **or** 2. Credit/Debit card **or** 3. Direct debit **(the name and address you give must match the information on your credit/Debit card/bank statement.)**

YOUR DETAILS (Please complete]

Title .... Christian name .... Surname ....
Address: ....
....
....
Postcode .... Daytime telephone no ....
Email: ....

- I enclose a cheque for the total amount of £..............
  payable to Hymns Ancient and Modern Ltd.
- To pay by credit/debit card please visit www.crucible.hymnsam.co.uk/subscriptions or contact us on 01603 785911

Ancient & Modern — Instruction to your bank or building society to pay by Direct Debit

Please fill in the whole form using a ball point pen and send to:
Hymns Ancient & Modern Ltd.

Name and full postal address of your bank or building society

To: The Manager   Bank/building society

Address

Postcode

Name(s) of account holder(s)

Bank/building society account number

Branch sort code

Service user number: 2 4 3 2 3 3

Reference

Instruction to your bank or building society
Please pay Hymns Ancient & Modern Ltd Direct Debits from the account detailed in this Instruction subject to the safeguards assured by the Direct Debit Guarantee. I understand that this Instruction may remain with Hymns Ancient & Modern Ltd and, if so, details will be passed electronically to my bank/building society.

Hymns Ancient & Modern Ltd, 13a Hellesdon Park Road, Norwich NR6 5DR

Signature(s)

Banks and building societies may not accept Direct Debit Instructions for some types of account.

This Guarantee should be detached and retained by the payer.

The Direct Debit Guarantee

- This Guarantee is offered by all banks and building societies that accept instructions to pay Direct Debits
- If there are any changes to the amount, date or frequency of your Direct Debit Hymns Ancient & Modern Ltd will notify you 10 working days in advance of your account being debited or as otherwise agreed. If you request Hymns Ancient & Modern Ltd to collect payment, confirmation of the amount and date will be given to you at the time of the request
- If an error is made in the payment of your Direct Debit, by Hymns Ancient & Modern Ltd or your bank or building society, you are entitled to a full and immediate refund of the amount paid from your bank or building society
  - If you receive a refund you are not entitled to, you must pay it back when Hymns Ancient & Modern Ltd asks you to
- You can cancel a Direct Debit at any time by simply contacting your bank or building society. Written confirmation may be required. Please also notify us

www.ingramcontent.com/pod-product-compliance
Ingram Content Group UK Ltd.
Pitfield, Milton Keynes, MK11 3LW, UK
UKHW042003230426
12048UKWH00009B/507